SECULAR ILLUSION
OR CHRISTIAN REALISM?

SECULAR ILLUSION OR CHRISTIAN REALISM?

by
D. R. DAVIES

First American Edition

NEW YORK
THE MACMILLAN COMPANY
1949

TO

ALFRED EDGAR AND MABEL GLOVER

WITH GRATITUDE AND AFFECTION

FOREWORD
BY THE LATE
ARCHBISHOP TEMPLE

IN this book Mr. D. R. Davies goes to the root of the trouble of the modern world. Essentially this is nothing other than the root of the world's trouble at any other time—the sinfulness of man. But in form this varies from age to age and Mr. Davies shows with penetrating analysis how completely the evil plant is one at every stage of its growth, while throwing light on its contemporary phase by the aid of modern psychology and the study of recent political events.

It will be hard for any reader to maintain any sort of complacency about our world in face of the analysis of it which is here convincingly presented. I hope that many will be led by it first to radical despair of solving the world's or their own problem apart from God self-manifested in Jesus Christ, and then to new confidence and enterprise through that manifestation.

CONTENTS

INTRODUCTION

TO anyone who understands the thought and spirit of the Bible, on which Christianity is based, nothing is more surprising or ridiculous than the way in which Christianity has come to stand for sentimentalism; for easy, superficial kindness; for what so many people call "trust in human nature." One reason for this is the utterly shallow and wrong way in which love has come to be regarded, and Christianity, as the religion of love, has suffered accordingly. Love, in the minds of most people, means merely to be kind and sympathetic; to be tolerant of everything; just "to kiss and make friends." Thus Christianity degenerates into sheer sentimentalism, because it teaches that by loving people you can make them good. That is, by persistent and continuous kindness, by never being angry, by unfailing patience and ignoring of wrong, you can win the world from evil to good. This is a caricature of the true, living Christianity. But it is this caricature which most non-Christians seem to have in their minds when they think of Christianity. It is also this caricature which many pacifist Christians seem to regard as New Testament Christianity.[1]

Now the idea, or theory, behind all this way of thinking —and all thinking implies a theory of some sort—is trust in human nature. It is the belief that deep down, when

[1] *Vide* C. J. Cadoux's *Christian Pacifism Re-examined.* (Basil Blackwell, Oxford, 1940.)

you come to rock-bottom, the human heart is good, loving and kind; that unselfishness is the deepest thing, the original thing, in human nature. *Evil is really an accident.* It is due to all sorts of causes—for example, to ignorance. If men and women only knew and understood better, there would be no more war or social evils. If they only learned from experience.[1] Or it may be due to man's animal origins, or to a wrong social system, as the Marxists and socialists generally teach. Fundamentally, human nature is good and therefore you can trust it to respond to kindness, patience and goodwill. Goodness is innate. Evil is acquired.

This theory has inspired a good deal of recent educational thinking and practice, and, what is more immediately disastrous, a good deal of political practice and policy. It has been the *idea* right at the back of the politics of appeasement. The idea has been camouflaged and disguised, but it has been there right enough. Hitler, fundamentally, was inspired by the unselfish passion for the welfare and progress of the German people; therefore he could be trusted. You could make a deal with him. We are now paying in costly practice the price of a wrong theory about human nature. History has taken over the argument from logic.

Now the point of central importance in all this, the point on which the reader must fasten, *is the way in which evil is thought of.* It is not radical—that is, not at the roots of the human heart. It is second-hand. It has come from outside the essential personality or ego of man—either from heredity or environment. Let us get at the essential

---

[1] *Vide* Mr. George Glasgow's *Diplomacy and God*, p. 6. (Longmans, Green. 1941.)

ego, and we shall be dealing with an angel. *Not* a devil. This is what trust in human nature finally comes to.

Not only is this trust in human nature not Christianity, it is the opposite and the completest negation of Christianity, as will be argued later in greater detail and thoroughness. Meanwhile, let us be absolutely clear on one point. Trust in human nature, which results in the most appalling sentimentalism and in the most incredible shallowness about life and history, may be true or false; may be a beautiful creed or not; but whatever it is, *it is not Christian*. On the contrary, it is the most utterly anti-Christian view of life and man which has ever appeared during the two thousand years of history since Christ. It severs the very lifeline of the Christian religion.

Whether Christianity be true or false, whether or not it has any further relevance to our world, it does not regard evil in man as an unfortunate accident, as a mere incident in history, which future progress will overcome. Evil in man is fundamental. That famous rock-bottom ego is devil, not angel. Hence, sentimental appeals to that subterranean gentleman will be useless, whether you clothe them in the jargon of new educational theory, or the elevated language of a philosophy. He will only grin and continue to make of life a hell and disaster. Nothing is to be gained from softening the absolute contrast or divergence between Christianity with its disbelief in the capacity of human nature to overcome evil, and the various creeds and beliefs (which for convenience' sake we may call Secularism or Humanism) which, in the last analysis, place their confidence in the power of human nature in itself to get rid of evil. These two are for ever contradictory, as far from each other as the east is from the west. They can no more be mixed or synthesised than fire and water, light and darkness, life and death. If we believe in man's power of self-salvation, we cannot possibly be Christian. We must be either Secularist or Christian. "Ye cannot serve God and Mammon."

Secular Illusion or Christian Realism? This is the supreme challenge to our generation, in which challenge there are summed up all the great issues at stake in the world to-day. Let us take the single issue of Dictatorship versus Democracy. If human nature is fundamentally good and not evil; if, that is to say, the Secularist is right and the Christian wrong, why not Dictatorship? If at rock-bottom man is to be trusted, what objection can there be to giving exceptional men absolute power to govern mankind? The most drunken of optimists even, the most wishy-washy of sentimentalists, cannot deny that the mass of mankind is still very undeveloped as compared with the exceptional minority. That fact is as plain as a pikestaff. Why not let the gifted few rule the roost? Down at bottom they are sound, and, after the necessary experimentation, they are sure to use absolute power for the good of their fellow-creatures, for their discipline and training in personal progress and moral advancement. Why not, *if in their ultimate ego there is goodness and unselfishness?* Given the assumption of the secularist, that is a sound argument. Stripped of its idealism, that was the argument of Plato. It is the philosophers who should be kings. Hitler is the incarnation of the secular illusion about man.

But suppose man is not to be trusted, even the most gifted? Suppose that down at the root there is not unselfishness, but the most persistent, untiring self-will? Then the argument against Dictatorship, even of the most gifted and exceptional, becomes absolute; for the more power you give to him, the more he is sure to abuse it. It was a Christian historian, Lord Acton, who said that "all power corrupts, absolute power corrupts absolutely." And that is the unvarying experience of man in every age. Popes may exercise power in the name of Christ. But that simple fact, as papal history abundantly proves, does not automatically protect the Papacy against the abuse of power.[1] Cromwell acquired absolute power in the name of Christ. Congregationalists would not argue that it was not a bad thing. Stalin started off with visions of working-class emancipation, but, having got absolute power, has created a tyranny greater than that of any Czar. No man can be trusted with power over his fellows, or as William Morris expressed it: "no man is good enough to be another man's master." Democracy is the search for the ideal check to power. Consciously or unconsciously, it is becoming aware that man is not good enough to exercise power uncontrolled.

So in this great challenge, Secular Illusion or Christian Realism, there is included the tragic issue of our time, and indeed the tragic issue of man's place in history itself. Christianity is a religion of tragedy. It faces the ugly and monstrous fact of the evil, the radical evil, of the human heart with unshrinking courage and unfailing hope. Whoever basks in the artificial sunshine of cloud-cuckoo land,

[1] The appalling cruelties and persecutions of which the new political religions have been guilty during the last twenty years have compelled me to judge papal abuses a little less harshly. The Inquisition, at its worst, was a gentle caress compared to the monstrosities inflicted on dissenting minorities by Nazism and Bolshevism. The profession of Christianity, even if it does nothing else, induces a sense of guilt at least.

the Christian does not. He must be a ruthless realist; for man is a poisoned reed. He is a creature to be overcome. Christianity indulges in no rosy day-dreams of man's career in this world. It is too much oppressed by the nightmare of the reality of man. That Christianity, therefore, should have become identified with sentimental optimism about human nature is the outstanding absurdity of modern thought. It has much more in common with the literature of Greek tragedy which flourished in the era of the breakdown of Greek society than with the sunny superficiality of the Renaissance.

But it is not enough merely to say that Christianity faces the ugly unvarnished facts of life without any attempt to whitewash them. The out-and-out cynic also does that. But no one, not even its worst enemy, accuses Christianity of being cynical. Christianity is distinguished by the fact that it envisages different and opposite things at the same time and in a single relationship. "Be ye wise as serpents," said Christ, "and innocent as doves." A union of opposites with a vengeance! One may be a serpent *or* a dove, but how can one be both at the same time? And yet that is precisely what Christianity achieves. Hence, when it looks to man and his evil heart in history, it sees the eternal God and His love in Christ at the same time. It faces the truth about man in the light of the truth about God. It sees human sin against the background of the divine love. To see man as he is in history, cruel, murderous, lustful of power and pelf, and to see only that, is to become cynical and disillusioned. And that breeds a curious sentimentalism of its own which is just as shallow as that of secular optimism. But "to see life steadily and see it whole," to see man in history and at

the same time to see God in Christ is to give life its proper
meaning and depth. It is to add a whole new dimension to
human thinking. The realism of Christianity has significance and profundity. It blinks nothing of "the terror of
things" and yet it remains supremely confident and hope-
ful; for its faith is rooted in a God who is both all-powerful and all-loving. In the last resort, therefore, it can
afford to dispense with all illusions, and more especially
with the secular illusion of our time.

CHAPTER I

The Modern Illusion about Man

I

THE more we think of what we called, in the introduction, "trust in human nature," reliance on man's capacity to abolish evil by education, applied science and social organisation, the more amazing it seems, or, as Alice in Wonderland put it, it becomes " curiouser and curiouser." During the last four hundred years, the whole of European thought has been increasingly infected by this gigantic illusion about human power. And so, what everybody thinks comes at last to be regarded as natural, however strange and unnatural it may be in cold fact. There is nothing so stupid or untrue that, if a sufficient number of people believe it, will not be considered to be the greatest wisdom. To us to-day, the belief in witchcraft is obviously idiotic. But at one time it was taken for granted. And contrary to the usual belief, its universal acceptance as a fact took place, not in the supposed "dark ages" of medieval religion, but at the beginnings of modern enlightenment. St. Boniface in the eighth century rejected it and belief in it was treated as a crime by the laws of Charlemagne. It was in the seventeenth century, when Galileo and Newton were popularising the methods of exact science, that the persecution of witches became widespread. And it is in an age which has witnessed the triumph of science over

1

religion and all other forms of culture that an illusion, greater even than witchcraft, has found universal acceptance. This does not mean that we regard science as a bad thing or that we should attempt to abolish it. We couldn't anyhow. It simply shows how science, like other forms of culture, also breeds its own superstitions. And of all the superstitions that have deluded mankind, none has been greater or more disastrous in its effects than the superstition of human omnipotence, the assumption that, finally, man will be able to abolish evil in all its forms.

The illusion is, for all practical purposes, universal. People and schools of thought who differ violently about everything else are agreed in believing in man's omnipotence. Let us take a single example. Heaven knows that there is an abyss of difference between Liberal Capitalism and Marxism. They are like two islands separated by wide, raging seas. But deep down beneath the turbulent waters, their lands join. Capitalism believes in private property; Marxism believes in its socialisation. Capitalism believes in profit; Marxism in direct use. Capitalism believes in individualism; Marxism in collectivism. Capitalism believes that society constitutes a single community; Marxism that it is a community comprised of conflicting classes. Capitalism believes in the national state; Marxism in a super-national fatherland. Capitalism believes in gradual social reform; Marxism in the seizure of political power by the working-class. And so on. Cat and dog. Adam Smith, the philosopher of Capitalism, taught that social welfare was the by-product of *individual* self-interest; Marx, the philosopher of Communism, taught that it was the by-product of *collective*, working-class self-interest. Differences enough, surely, between these two.

And yet they are both at one in their assumption that Utopia is possible, that sometime, here on earth, all social evils will be abolished, and there will emerge a perfect society. Liberal Capitalism, in its golden age before 1914, looked forward to a continuous, steady progress. More and more wealth would be accumulated; profits and wages would become even greater; men would grow happier and happier; poverty and war would ultimately disappear; more and more machines would relieve men of heavy labour and so give them increasing leisure. The process was already under way. Time—that was all that was necessary; and patience, of course. Rome was not built in a day. But the point was that Utopia was already in the making.

Marxism was a little bit more realistic. It was more aware of the irrationality in man's make-up, and so realised the need for revolution. Utopia, said Capitalism, has already begun. Marxism said Utopia would not begin until after the social revolution. Simply a difference in date! Society is a conflict between classes for the product of industry. In capitalist society, the capitalist class owns the means of production, but, fortunately, Capitalism is creating its own destroyer. It is "its own gravedigger."[1] It makes the working-class stronger until, one glorious day, it will capture political power—army, police, civil service, press, the legal system, etc.—then the process of Utopia will begin. "On the morrow of the social revolution," wrote Engels, Marx's fellow-worker, "mankind will rise out of the kingdom of necessity into the kingdom

[1] *Capital*, Vol. I, pp. 836-7. (Kerr and Co., Chicago.)

of freedom." So beautifully simple! Destroy the capitalist class, and the working-class will be free to tackle the job of making heaven upon earth. There is not a hint of any doubt about capacity to do it. Both capitalist and Marxist are singing the same theme-song. They differ merely in their variations.

In passing, let the reader note two points.

First, something has gone wrong somewhere with the schemes of both Capitalism and of Marxism. Not even Adam Smith could argue that a Nazified Europe constitutes Utopia. In fact we are further away from Utopia to-day than ever. And it is very doubtful if this generation can be persuaded by political magicians that it is only just round the corner. And the social revolution, which really did happen in 1917, seems to have gone awry. It seems to be turning into a tyranny much worse than Capitalism. And it was to patriotism, not to world revolution, that Stalin made his appeal in the war against Germany.

Something went wrong somewhere. But where?

The second thing to note is the really damnable cruelty and egoism of both the capitalist and the Marxist view of history. Both place Utopia in a future more or less distant, when a late generation of men and women will enjoy the full fruits of the suffering and tragedy of all those who have gone before. But what about the millions who lived and died, "their heritage a sunless day"? Were they just flies on the wheel of fate? Was it their destiny simply to suffer that a mere handful, comparatively, should lord it in splendid ease over history and the world? To this problem neither Capitalism nor Marxism gives any answer. Indeed they do not recognise it. Christianity does recognise it and answer it in its doctrine of the resurrection of the dead.

This fundamental agreement about human nature between two such violently opposed systems of thought as Capitalism and Marxism extends over the whole field of modern life and belief. It has even penetrated the Church and her theology, with the result that men calling themselves Christian had an agreement with the bitterest opponents of Christianity which was more profound than their disagreements from them. Liberal Protestantism, of which Harnack, the great German New Testament scholar and Church historian, was an outstanding figure, did away with man's need of a redeemer. Need of a teacher, a guide, a prophet, a reformer—yes. But a *redeemer*, of one to do something of which man himself, unaided, is incapable? No. Redemption is an automatic, biological process. Christ is one of the highlights in the development of man from jellyfish to angel. Thus Harnack, a Christian, was in fundamental agreement with Bernstein, a Marxist, who regarded Christianity as the greatest enemy of social progress; for they both believed in man's power to redeem himself. Agreement on that question makes disagreement on other points pretty well meaningless and insignificant. It is like people who are going to the same place in a double-decker bus quarrelling whether they shall sit upstairs or down.

II

How has the modern world achieved so profound a self-deception?

In the long, eventful history of Europe since the death of Christ very many great changes have taken place, not only in the outward happenings and structure of society —these, after all, are not of the first importance, though very important—but also, and more significantly, in the ideas, attitudes and purposes of the minds of men. Among the greatest of these changes was the complex of events and ideas which go under the names of Renaissance and Reformation. In these world-shaking movements, humanity struck its tents and went on the march. In them, human pride, which throughout the medieval period had been held on a leash, broke loose and began its career of gigantic inflation. Not least active in the breaking of the shackles was the Papacy itself, with its monstrous claims and its terrible corruption. The Reformation, which resulted in the subordination of the Church to the national state, was a European disaster, but a necessary disaster, made so by Rome.

In the Renaissance of the fifteenth century, which was a degeneration of the true Renaissance in the twelfth century,[1] Europe broke away from the domination of Catholicism, which, for all its defects, constantly reminded man of his subordination to God. So long as the idea of God as supreme was a conscious *natural* idea in the minds of men pride was held on a chain and was aware of its limitations. When that began to get dim, as it did in the second Renaissance, European man became intoxicated with the sense of his own creative power. It was an era of tremendous release. But it was an illusion,

[1] *Vide* Mr. Lewis Mumford's very fine study, *The Culture of Cities* (Secker and Warburg. Cheap edition, 1940), pp. 73-78, for a really illuminating discussion of this question. "The so-called Renascence that followed (the twelfth century one) in the fifteenth century was rather in the nature of an illusory belief on the part of its contemporaries: they mistook the brilliant spray of the falling rocket for the energy that had originally lifted it into the air" (pp. 75-6).

though it has taken Europe nearly four hundred years to realise it; for release from the restraining idea of the centrality and supremacy of God has resulted in the infinitely worse slavery of state and mechanism. The uneasy tension between Church and Empire in medieval Europe prevented political power from ever becoming absolute. The power claiming sovereignty over men itself recognised a still greater sovereignty, unlike the modern dictatorships which acknowledge no superior. Can we imagine, for instance, in Germany to-day the oath of allegiance which the people swore to their kings in Aragon: "We, who are as good as you, swear to you, who are not better than we, to accept you as our king and sovereign lord, provided that you observe all our liberties and laws; but if not, then not"? Human power, whether political or social, was never absolute.

But with the rise of science and national sovereignty, there grew apace, though quite unconsciously, the superstition of human omnipotence. Perhaps there was some excuse for it; for by means of applied science, man made astonishing conquests over time and space. In fact, if not in theory, man forgot his limitations, that, after all, he too was but a creature.[1] Modern Europe is the history of the expansion of human pride from irritable awareness of limitation to supreme arrogance. It is the story of the growth of an illusion, the most disastrous in the entire history of mankind. We can trace it in the development

---

[1] "With the quest for financial and political power, the notion of limits disappeared—limits on numbers, limits on wealth, limits on population growth, limits on urban expansion; on the contrary, quantitative expansion became predominant. The merchant cannot be too rich; the state cannot possess too much territory; the city cannot become too big." (Mumford, *op. cit.*, p. 93.)

of nationality, of science and capitalism, of philosophy and theology. In the result, the characteristic dominant beliefs of medieval Europe have been replaced by exactly opposite ones. This world of time is no longer a place of pilgrimage—it has become a place of achievement and fulfilment. This world is no longer a dependency on another world—it has become self-contained and self-sufficing. Man no longer looks for heaven beyond time and space—he expects it here. No "pie in the sky" any more, but roast joints on earth. From uneasy awareness of incompleteness, limitation and frustration, modern man has advanced to an obsession of self-confidence. This is "the great illusion."

It takes to-day three main forms.

First, the social form, which is belief in the power of man to create Utopia here on earth. In this form, the illusion tends too readily to confuse technical possibility with moral capacity. Technically—so far, that is, as control over matter is concerned—there is no doubt that at some future time it will become possible to ensure the *material* conditions of a completely harmonious and continuously progressive society. Those conditions have not yet been achieved, even in advanced industrial communities, in spite of the popular, too easy talk of "an age of plenty." And the war, with its large-scale destruction, will seriously postpone it. Europe, at least, will have to face the necessity, not of an economics of plenty, but an economics of sacrifice, for a long time ahead. "No matter how long the present war lasts or what its outcome may be, life on this planet will be difficult for another two generations: probably at least for another century. . . . Recovery from this poisoned state will not come fast. . . .

After what has happened in Europe and Asia during the past decade, no human being has a right to hope for automatic improvements or compensation."[1]

But technical achievement is not the same thing as moral realisation. Without the moral the technical is frustrated. For example, our technical resources make possible a weekly consumption per capita of at least two lbs. of butter, two lbs. of jam, three lbs. of meat, four lbs. of dates or dried fruits, and twenty oranges.[2] But we only eat two ounces of butter, two ounces of jam, sixteen ounces of meat and no oranges or dates. Why? The war, which represents the moral failure of society, frustrates the technical. The productive capacity which goes into butter, meat, etc., is diverted to armaments. "Guns instead of butter," as Goering said, who has compelled the world to follow suit. It is the inability of man in the moral realm which will always prevent him enjoying the full increment of his creative, technical power. In other words, the belief that Utopia is possible for unredeemed human nature is sheer delusion.

The second form of the secular illusion is the psychological: that by means of psycho-analysis it is possible to change the permanent, underlying condition of the human soul, which is the divided mind, disintegration of mind, heart and will, the basic inner conflict of personality. Psycho-analysis may and does reveal the mechanism of disintegration; it may and does show how it operates. But it does not transform the soul from division into unity. When the analyst has done his best, conflict

[1] Lewis Mumford's *Faith for Living* (Secker and Warburg, 1941) p. 145.
[2] *Vide* Mr. Frank Verulam: *Product for the People.* (Lawrence and Wishart, 1940.)

remains—frequently it becomes worse. To make the personality an integrated harmony is beyond human power.

The third form taken by the illusion is the moral or spiritual: that by educational progress, man's sense of guilt can be eradicated. This is the greatest delusion of all. Modern neurosis, which is a new disease, is largely the result of trying to pretend that guilt has vanished. Guilt is as permanent a reality as death, and comes from the same source, which the New Testament describes as *Sin*. "For the wages of sin is death." The sense of guilt, to which the whole of life testifies in every age and clime, is irremovable by man himself.

III

The most disturbing practical consequence of the secular illusion about human nature in social and political life is that it leads to an appalling under-estimation of the seriousness of the problems facing mankind. The modern view of man is so shallow that it constantly fails to realise the depth and the scale and the enormity of the human problem. Its optimism is so superficial that it assumes that the difficulty of man's situation in history can be more easily resolved than in sober fact it ever can be. This inadequate realisation of what we are dealing with—constantly mistaking the dragon for a worm, the giant for a dwarf—involves us in the contradiction *that we solve our existing problems at the cost of creating new and still more difficult problems*. In other words, man does not solve the problem: he merely changes its form. A detailed discussion of this fact would demand a volume in itself. We must be content merely to illustrate it.

Over thirty years ago (if I may be permitted a personal

confession), in common with thousands of other utopian socialists, I looked forward with certainty to the establishment of socialism in a mere matter of years. The first lecture I delivered, on an I.L.P. platform, was on the subject, "The First Monday Morning under Socialism." With the true Celtic touch, I painted a gorgeous picture of a Britain where the grass would always be green, the cows' udders would always be full, where sparrows would lay ostrich eggs; where, in short, life would be a lovely summer idyll. Thirty years ago! And here I am, to mention one little circumstance, separated from my family, whom I have had to evacuate for safety from sudden death and mutilation. My summer dream has turned into a nightmare, which is a parable of miscalculated human nature. It was going to be so simple. A few years of propaganda to wake up the workers. A few general elections—and behold a majority for socialism! The job was done! It was going to be as easy as that. "But surely," the reader may be tempted to argue, "surely, society is not so simple and optimistic as all that." Well, let us see.

In 1789, when the French people shovelled the absolute monarchy of the Bourbons and the whole *ancien régime* into the dustbin of history, they cleared the arena, as they thought, for a new society of equality, liberty and fraternity. An entrancing vision! Little did they think they were laying the foundations for Fascism and a new slavery, compared to which the despotism of Louis XVI was a blessing. They elected 632 representatives to the National Assembly, who were given the task of making a Constitution for the new France, in which all citizens were to be equal(!), free(!) and brotherly(!). *It was all going to be done in a fortnight.*[1] A bunch of political amateurs and psychological ignoramuses, drunk with the new wine of popular rights, which had been served to them by Rousseau and the Encyclopedists, succeeded at last, after interminable talking and wrangling, in making a Constitution which led immediately to Napoleon's domestic tyranny and foreign aggression. Equality! Liberty! Fraternity!

"We have seen that almost all the *cahiers* (*i.e.* lists of complaints and reforms) expressed a desire for political self-government, and that the *cahiers* of the Third Estate at least demanded the making of a new Constitution. Many of the *cahiers* entered into some detail regarding its provisions. Many also required that its principles should be enacted before any supply was granted to the Crown. As soon, therefore, as the fusion of the Orders had been effected, the Assembly undertook to give France a Constitution. The task seemed light, for the spirit of the majority was confident to excess. 'Politics,' said Sieyès, 'is a science which I believe myself to have completed.' 'The Constitution,' said Barère, 'is already made in the minds of all. There can be no laborious travail here; the Constitution is perhaps the work of a day, because it is the result of the enlightenment of an age.' "[2]

When it became clear that surrounding states did not share the French enthusiasm for equality and liberty and fraternity, the Assembly prepared with zealous passion for war. And they did a new thing, which has proved to

---

[1] *Vide Cambridge Modern History*, Vol. 8, Chapters 1-7, for the details. The whole story, with its incredible levity, were it not so profound a tragedy, especially in view of France's collapse in June 1940, would be first-class comic opera.

[2] *Ibid.*, p. 176.

be one of Europe's greatest curses. They introduced the
levée en masse, Conscription. It was the New Democracy,
France, not the Old Despotism, Prussia, that first established Conscription. Prussia later improved upon it and
France suffered the recoil in 1870 and a still greater one
in 1940. And Conscription, if you please, was to be the
instrument of Europe's emancipation from all despots!
God must have a grim sense of humour. The draft law
introducing the measure in the Assembly evoked such
mad enthusiasm, that Barère had to read it twice. He was
encored like any fat, popular opera tenor. And he re-
sponded: "Single men will fight in the front line. Married
men will make munitions and man the supply services.
Women will make the uniforms and serve in the hospitals.
Children will assist the women by cutting and measuring
cloth. And old men will harangue the masses, and preach
hatred of kings so as to unite free peoples." And out of
all this will be born a new Europe of liberty!

This requires no argument. History has given the
answer. France certainly solved the problem of a decaying Feudalism and an inefficient monarchy, but in doing
so prepared a new and infinitely greater problem. Instead
of Feudalism, we have Fascism. The miscalculation of
the terrific difficulties involved in creating a democratic
state was fantastic. My dream of socialism compared
with the National Assembly's prancing anticipations was
that of a seasoned cynic.

The nineteenth and twentieth centuries, with less excuse
than the eighteenth, have in practice proved to be just as
fantastic in their shallow appreciation of the problem
involved. The Marxist anticipation of a classless society
as the result of a working-class revolution (itself a chimera

as far as Western Europe is concerned) is as empty as the French dream. Lenin's famous dictum is the last word in superficiality: "socialism is sovietisation plus electrification." A new society is merely a matter of political power plus technique! Could anything be more childishly naïve?

After the last war, Dr. William Adams Brown, a leading American Liberal Protestant, innocently asks why, since nations will co-operate to fight disease, they will not co-operate to abolish war.[1] Note the culpable failure to understand the nature of war, which is put into the same category as malaria or yellow fever. There is an example of Liberal Protestantism's appreciation of human nature —about two inches deep.

A similar superficiality is rampant in relation to the current problem of Fascism and the condition of Europe. Sir Robert Vansittart reduces it to the simple dimensions of the uniquely evil character of the German people, whom he dismisses as "butcher birds."[2] As though Germany is a wolf in the midst of lambs! There certainly is a German problem. Not to realise that is the unrealism of the political left. But it is a basic element of a far wider problem. Dr. Buchman of the Oxford Group goes to the other extreme of superficialism, and thinks that if you could convert Hitler or Mussolini to his degenerate brand of Christianity, Europe would be set miraculously right.

The fundamental error in all this is the grandiose illusion that human nature in its present condition of radical self-will has the power either to create permanent institutions or to cure itself of its basic egoism.

[1] *Vide Pathways to Certainty.* (Hodder and Stoughton.)
[2] *Vide Black Record.*

CHAPTER II

The Revelation of War

HOW does this modern assumption about man—
for it is no more than an assumption, and moreover, a purely gratuitous assumption—fare in
the presence of history and experience? What
does it look like in the light of unemotional, unromantic
fact? One of the paradoxes of life is, of course, the ob-
stinacy with which people cling to ideas and beliefs
against which daily experience screams denial. Therefore,
to demonstrate the denial of history does not necessarily
mean that men will cease to believe in the myth of collective omnipotence; for the roots of human pride go deeper
than history, and its destruction will require bombard-
ment from guns very much heavier than any in the
artillery of mere logic. But, at least, something is gained
if it can be shown that, in the world of objective, concrete
fact, there is not a shadow of justification for man's
self-confidence. On the contrary, the evidence against it
is conclusive.

And for this purpose nothing is so illuminating as a
study of the fact of war as a social institution. War is the
final logic of self-will. Its essence and significance as conflict cannot be disguised or rationalised, which does not
mean, of course, that the motives for waging it or resort-
ing to it cannot be rationalised. They always are. The
world will always be able to persuade itself that its reasons
for doing evil are good. That is a part of its sinful heritage.

15

But war is one of the few institutions which society regards as a *necessary* evil. Other institutions it thinks of as necessary but good. Still others it thinks of as evil but not necessary. War almost alone is thought of as both evil and necessary. In the development of war, therefore, we can judge best the capacity of human nature. What has the world made of war, of this thing which it recognises as evil?

I

Right at the threshold of our investigation, we meet with a profound contradiction.

Now it is a fact that we think of war as abnormal, exceptional, strange. Peace, we imagine, is the normal, ordinary condition of society. War is an unfortunate interruption of peace, and is pursued in order to gain peace and preserve it. But the truth of the matter is exactly the opposite. *War is the normal condition of society, peace the abnormal.* Whether we define the word "abnormal" in the time sense as meaning occasional, happening infrequently, or in the psychological sense as meaning exceptional, a departure from character, a violation and contradiction of ordinary being, then unquestionably, war is a normal activity in human history, that is, in the history of civilised man. The more civilised man becomes, the more warlike he also becomes, and—a point of decisive importance—the more destructive, inhuman and immoral does war become in character. It is at least as true to say that peace is the pursuit of war as to say that war is the pursuit of peace. The dictum of Clausewitz that war is the prosecution of politics by other means could as justifiably be rendered as that politics is the prosecution of war by other means. The facts leave no reasonable room for doubt.

Let us, to begin with, examine the assertion that war is due to the survival of the animal in man and to the operation of his "savage" instincts. War, we are told, is "natural" to man, which is so nearly true, and yet so far from the truth. War is second nature to man, uniquely so. It is the consequence of the nature which he acquired by his deliberate rebellion against dependence upon God. War is not part of the original nature with which God endowed man. It became part of the nature he made for himself by his exercise of self-will against the divine will. War, therefore, is uniquely human, not animal. It is the result of mind and will, not of instinct. As Montaigne put it in one of his essays, "war is a specific characteristic of the human species." Was it not Lord Shaftesbury who maintained, in reply to Hobbes' statement that "man is a wolf to his fellow-man," that it was an insult to the wolf, that no wolf would treat his fellow-wolf as man treats his fellow-man?

Mutual extermination, which presumably would be regarded as the equivalent among animals of war in the human species, is by no means a law in the animal world.[1] Solidarity and co-operation have been, at least, equally as important. Besides, success in the struggle for existence has not always been gained by the more voracious beasts. On the contrary, it has frequently been gained by the less cruel and voracious. There is no justification for shifting the responsibility for war from mind to animal instinct.

[1] For details, read Kropotkin's *Mutual Aid*, Novicow's *La Critique de Darwinisme Social* and P. C. Mitchell's *Darwinism and War*, and Professor J. A. Thompson's popular studies, particularly his *Darwinism and Human Life*.

Neither does the theory of the blood-thirstiness of the primitive savage fare any better. The patient researches of anthropologists like Westermarck during the last twenty years have conclusively proved that primitive man was not at all like a voracious beast. For one thing, he lacked the necessary dynamic urge, which was one reason why he did not enter on a career of civilisation. War is a product of civilisation, of developing, progressive society. There is good reason for believing that primitive man was a vegetarian, not a carnivore.[1]

Now in the history of civilisation itself, war is a normal activity, a regular feature of the landscape, so to speak. Prof. Pitrim Sorokin[2] has amassed a great wealth of facts, which dispose of the myth that war tends to diminish as civilisation advances. He also shows clearly that man has spent more time in waging wars than in preserving peace. "G. Valbert, on the basis of the computation of the Moscow Gazette, says that 'from the year 1496 B.C. to A.D. 1861, in 3,358 years, there were 227 years of peace and 3,130 years of war, or thirteen years of war to every year of peace. Within the last three centuries there have been 286 wars in Europe.' He adds further that 'from the year 1500 B.C. to A.D. 1860 more than 8,000 treaties of peace, which were meant to remain in force for ever, were concluded. The average time they remained in force was two years.' Valbert, G., in the *Revue des Deux Mondes*, April 1894, p. 692."[3]

Excluding colonial wars, which arose out of the power-

---

[1] *Vide* Novicow's book referred to in preceding note.
[2] *Vide Contemporary Sociological Theories* (Harrap and Co., 1928), pp. 309-356. I am greatly indebted to this invaluable study both for facts and for guidance in further reading.
[3] *Ibid.*, p. 325.

politics of European states, of which there have been over seventy since 1860, in the eighty years since the above computation was made, there have been several major wars which in scale and significance greatly exceeded the more numerous wars before 1860. To mention but a few of them, there were the three wars of Prussian aggression in 1864, 1866, and 1870; the Russo-Turkish War of 1877; the Italian conflict with Turkey; the two Balkan wars, 1911-13; the Russo-Japanese War, 1905-6; the first World War in 1914-18; and now the second World War, 1939-?. Ten major wars in eighty years in Europe, or involving European powers. This takes no account of the armed conflicts of non-European powers, the civil wars, and revolutions. It is absolutely staggering to reflect (what is probably the truth) that, during the 6,000 years of the history of civilisation, the world has not known one single year in which a war between some country or other was not being fought. Not a single year in this period to which we can point and say: "In that year, the whole world was at peace."

We can look at the facts in another way, from the angle of the separate European countries. Mr. F. A. Woods and Mr. G. Bodart[1] have made an exhaustive analysis of the war-activities of twelve European states, and their conclusions are practically the same. Since the year 1100, England has spent half the period in fighting wars of different kinds, France nearly half, Austria-Hungary three-quarters, Russia three-quarters, and Prussia about one-quarter of the period since 1600 in war. A tabular presentation is given on p. 20.[2]

[1] Quoted by Sorokin, *ibid.*, p. 324.
[2] *Vide* Sorokin, *ibid.*, p. 324.

Thus civilised man has spent most of his time in waging war—that is, in doing something which he knows and admits to be evil. War, therefore, can hardly be called abnormal. The thing to which we give the greater portion of our time and energy ceases to be exceptional and becomes more or less habitual. De Maistre saw as much when he wrote that "in a certain sense war is an habitual condition of the human race."

NUMBER OF YEARS SPENT IN WAR IN EACH SPECIFIED CENTURY BY EACH SPECIFIED COUNTRY

Country	1100–1200	1201–1300	1301–1400	1401–1500	1501–1600	1601–1700	1701–1800	1801–1900
England .	54	36	65	57	54·5	43·5	55·5	53·5
France .	36·5	49	43	52·5	60·5	46·5	50·5	35
Austria .					75·5	73·5	48·5	13·5
Austria-Hungary						77	59	25
Russia .					78·5	57·5	49·5	53
Turkey .					80·5	89	23	39·5
Spain .					73	82	48·5	53·5
Poland .					55	68	22·5	
Prussia .						58·5	31	13
Holland .						62·5	29·5	14·5
Sweden .					50·5	50	29·5	6·5

War has become increasingly a habit in the modern world, seeing that the interregnum of peace is devoted to preparation for the next war. Since the eighteenth century Europe has never been free either of an actual war or preparing for one. And the preparation for war is just as significant as war itself, as the case of Prussia proves. Judging by the figures alone, it would seem that Prussia was the least militant state in the nineteenth century. But we know better to our grave cost. Since Bismarck initiated the policy of uniting Germany by "blood and iron," Prussia, with the added power of the German states, has become the most militarist state in the world, the modern Assyria, a veritable "butcher bird" among nations. There began with Bismarck a crescendo of Prussian militarism which in Hitler roared to a double fortissimo. Between 1864 and 1900, Prussia's three wars lasted barely two years, but her constantly growing armaments kept Europe in a fever of insecurity. She was always fighting either a war of guns or a war of nerves, which Hitler developed into a fine art. To a lesser degree, the same was true of the rest of Europe. War had become a fundamental part of its psychology. How profoundly wrong, then, is the popular way of thinking of war as occasional or abnormal. Up to the present, it has been one of the most enduring of all social institutions, one of human nature's most characteristic expressions. We shall discuss the significance of this at a later stage of the argument.

II

War, let it be repeated, is almost the only institution which, since the founding of Christianity, has been looked upon as a necessary evil. It is also, practically, the only institution which has undergone no essential change of form. It remains a permanent problem for mankind, becoming greater for each succeeding generation—that is, becoming *more* intractable, *less* soluble. Contrary to the usual expectation, the danger of war has not diminished with the so-called progress of the world. On the contrary, it has increased. Occasions of war are greater in our advanced technical society than in any previous civilisation

—and also fraught with greater possibilities of universal disaster. For the first time in the history of mankind, the evil of war threatens the whole of humanity with destruction. It is to this that all the glory and creative power of man has at last arrived. And the problem of war presents itself to the twentieth century in essentially the same form as it did in the first—the final inability to compromise the claims of opposing egoisms.

Social progress, which is, of course, an objective fact in history, does not mean that the world is growing morally better. A really strong case can be made for the thesis that it is becoming worse. It certainly is not getting better. Progress does not mean moral and spiritual amelioration. If it did, then it would mean that society was gradually getting rid of the various social ills that have afflicted it throughout the course of its history. But that is precisely what it is *not* doing. There is hardly one social evil, for example, which cursed the ancient world, which does not exist to-day—*in a different form*. Take slavery as an example. Slavery (chattel slavery—that is, legal ownership of the person) was a particular social form for the exploitation of labour. The real evil of slavery was the exploitation. Now it is true that modern society has abolished that particular form of exploitation.[1] But it has substituted for it its own native form for doing the same

[1] Nazi Germany is reintroducing even the ancient form. Note its action in Poland and Yugo-Slavia of transporting wholesale thousands of men to labour in Germany for "iron wages"—for just sufficient to enable them to continue working, or, in Mr. Mumford's phrase, "to get them to return to the job." In the eighteenth century, capitalist Europe did the same thing to the negroes. That is, technical progress galvanised a decaying institution into new life. *Vide* Toynbee's *A Study of History* (Oxford University Press), Vol. IV (1939), pp. 137-141.

thing. Not to realise this is a colossal self-deception. In capitalist society, a more intense process of exploiting labour is carried on by means of the new form of wage-slavery, of treating labour (living men and women) *as a commodity*. And on the whole, it is probably true to say that the lot of the ancient slave was no worse than that of the de-classed modern worker. In any case, an honest recognition of the facts makes it quite clear that the evil of the social and economic exploitation of labour, which the ancient world practised through chattel slavery, is effected by the modern world through wage-slavery and semi-chattel-slavery (as in Kenya, Shanghai, India, etc.). A similar analysis of prostitution, child exposure, and other ancient evils would reveal a similar conclusion.

Thus social progress, in fact, consists, not of a process of abolishing evils, but of changing their form. Chattel slavery becomes serfdom, and serfdom becomes wage-slavery. Roman absolutism becomes Holy Roman, which, in due course, becomes national sovereignty, which threatens to end in a new form of absolutism infinitely worse than either Roman or Holy Roman. The social form changes, but the content, the substance, of the form abides.

The single exception of this process is war. It abides both in substance and in form. This is a fact of very profound significance. The only change which war has undergone is a change for the worse in every respect. It has become more pervasive, more destructive, more disastrous for humanity as a whole. Its continuance may literally mean the extermination of mankind. Such a possibility has never existed before; for never before has mankind been one society. But to-day, for good or ill, mankind constitutes a single community. The Indian peasant is a part of the same organism as the European aristocrat. The Egyptian fellaheen is a cell in the same body as the American or British bourgeoisie. Both are now involved in a common destiny or doom. This is the technical achievement of Capitalism, which has thrown down the barriers separating peoples from one another, and which enabled them to live, behind mountain range or ocean rampart, their own hermetically sealed communal existence. The tribal Abyssinian shares in the blessings of a scientific civilisation through his taste of poison-gas.

This is why isolation is the dream of diseased egoists. There is no possibility of immunity for anybody either in war or social evil in the world of to-day. The Lindberghs and Wheelers of the world are the most desperately neurotic of all sick souls, being incapable of adapting themselves to reality. They are living in a super-fantastic dream world of their own, suffering from a veritable elephantiasis of egoism. And they have a following of 30 per cent. in the United States.[1] Such are the souls that a society breeds which has rejected the Christian value of life. It is impossible to imagine such people in medieval Europe.

Now there must surely be something radically wrong with human nature, when the sum total of its creative genius is to make its greatest social problem more and more incapable of solution: this is what has actually happened. All the gains and the progress of modern Europe have resulted in increasing the scale and depth of the

[1] So stated Mr. Raymond Gram Swing in the *Sunday Express* of July 6th, 1941. Mr. Swing is known as one of the most sober and responsible of publicists.

problem. Something wrong there! It reveals the most terrible of all moral contradictions. *It shows how even the good of which human nature is undoubtedly capable seems to end in evil.* We can illustrate this grim fact by a consideration of a few typical modern advantages.

First of all, there is education.

Leaving on one side any discussion of what true education is, and confining ourselves to its most elementary aspect as simple literacy, ability to read and write, universal education, an undoubtedly good thing, has enormously increased the evil of war. It has made it easier to harness the power of masses to the pursuit of war. It has also intensified the cruelty and ruthlessness with which war is waged. The wars of kings and dynasties in the eighteenth century were comparatively gentlemanly affairs compared to the twentieth century wars of peoples.

It is universal literacy, the result of the Education Act of 1870, that made possible the rise of the modern Press, which began with the publication of Alfred Harmsworth's *Daily Mail*. So gradually we witnessed the standardisation of news and opinion, mass production of emotions and ideas. Millions of people came to read the same lies and half-truths. One of the earliest fruits of popular education was the mafficking of the Boer War. There are many who think to-day, forty years after the event, that the Boer War was a war of naked aggression against a small people. But it was one of the most popular of all wars in British history. The passionate support of aggression was one of the consequences of everybody being able to read. Popular Press and popular education developed together and conditioned each other. By the careful doctoring of news, by the skilful presentation of half-truths, it became possible to infect a whole world with a passion for aggression. Something which in itself is good works out to evil consequences. Mr. Arnold Toynbee gives a striking confirmation of this in his really profound survey of history:[1] "These revolutionary reactions to the impact of Democracy upon Education, like the revolutionary reactions to the impact of Industry upon Private Property, have found their weapon in the 'totalitarian State'; and in Communist Russia and Fascist Italy and National Socialist Germany the press-lord and the cinema-lord have been the first members of the Capitalist tribe to be deprived of their ill-gotten and ill-used power by revolutionary violence. Yet, here again, the revolutionary remedy may prove still worse than the monstrous disease; for, in all these 'totalitarian' states, the means by which the masses have been delivered from the curse of mental exploitation for private profit has been the confiscation and manipulation of the Press and the Cinema by the Government. The elaborate and ingenious machinery for the mass-enslavement of elementarily educated minds, which was invented in the 19th century for the sake of private commercial profit under a régime of *laisser faire*, has here simply been taken over *in toto* by the rulers of states who have decided to employ these mental appliances for their own factious political purposes; and although their intellectual tyranny may be less sordid in its aims it is more crushing and more pervasive in its incidence than the tyranny of the private entrepreneurs into whose shoes the propaganda departments of the 'totalitarian' Governments have stepped."

Our second example is taken from Broadcasting, the

[1] *Vide A Study of History*, Vol. IX, p. 196.

really paradoxical result of which is to make truth very difficult of access to the masses!

The invention of wireless is one of the most striking manifestations of the dynamic, creative genius of man. By means of it, the conquest of both time and space is made possible. There is something positively uncanny in the thought that as soon as an event happens, say at one end of the world, news of it is flashed to the other end. Even as late as the Napoleonic wars, there was frequently an interval of weeks and months between the fighting of a battle and the communication of the result. But now the results can be known all over the world within a matter of minutes. This means, among many other things, a greater communion of life for the whole of mankind. The world is actually participating, *at the same time*, in the same experience. For good and ill, humanity is being inspired or poisoned at the same moment. Wireless is a powerful destroyer of spiritual and psychological privilege.

Now the possibilities of such an achievement in the dissemination and communication of truth and fact are obvious. It can make culture accessible to everybody. The best and the noblest products of the human mind in music, art, and literature and drama can be converted into current coin. Thirty years ago, as a boy in South Wales, the nine symphonies of Beethoven, for example, were only names to me. It was impossible to hear them. Wireless has made it possible to transform the humblest, poorest cottage kitchen into a concert-hall. And so with all the rest of the fruits of genius. The profoundest thought, the most elevated musical composition, the greatest drama can all become the raw material of personal development and education for everybody. It can bring about a degree of personal contact between the creative thinker, the leader, the pioneering minority, and the masses. For the first time, the forty millions odd of our people have all heard the voice of Britain's premier.

But these truly marvellous possibilities, at the same time, work to the corroding and darkening of masses. Without the wireless, Hitlerism, for example, would have been impossible. The instrument which is able to secure the triumph of culture is in fact bringing about its destruction over the larger part of Europe. How has it come about that so highly civilised a people and so moral a people as the Germans have come to tolerate and support a régime which is the denial of every good value in its own tradition? The answer is to be found in one word —Broadcasting. With the supreme political genius which characterises him, Hitler long ago saw and grasped the potentialities of broadcasting as a political instrument.[1] He has merely perfected a method clumsily practised by governments everywhere. That Hitler is our example for discussion does not mean that the prostitution of broadcasting is a German or even a Fascist monopoly. This is a crime to which no government can plead "Not Guilty."

What, in fact, has happened?

By exercising an absolute monopoly of broadcasting— and in doing this Hitler went the whole hog where other Governments only went part of the hog—Hitler ensured that the people should hear nothing except his own version of things. And by dint of constant repetition, he succeeded in making people believe that black was white. He perfected the methods of capitalist advertisement.

[1] *Vide* Rauschning's *Hitler Speaks.*

That is to say, he applied to politics a method of communication which a secular, capitalist, anti-Christian society had enthusiastically sanctioned in the holy cause of profit and commercial progress. It was capitalist advertisement that invented the art of making lies and half-truths look like truth. Hitler is the capitalist chicken coming home to roost—no longer a chicken, but a vulture, a monster bird of prey. The method by which you persuade a gullible public that somebody's water and powder are a powerful tonic can convince the same public that Jews or Marxists or Liberals or Catholics are the root of all evil in the state. A public subjected for a generation to the screaming arts of capitalist advertisement has been made suitably receptive to Hitler propaganda. Its mind has been so soused, doped, and enfeebled that it cannot summon up the necessary energy to distinguish between obvious lies and simple facts. It can fall at last for the obvious absurdity that a nation of 15,000,000 is a menace to a powerful people of 70,000,000. That is what Hitler meant when he said that people fall more easily to the big lie than to the petty one. He understood only too well the mentality which capitalist advertisement had created.[1]

Hitler rigidly excluded every point of view except his own. His high-powered and numerous radio stations poured forth a flood of propaganda, day after day, night after night, to convince the German people that they would have won the last war except for Jews and Marxists; that the Allies, through the maintenance of the Versailles Peace Treaty, were bent on their subjection;

[1] This fact should convince us that responsibility for the present state of Europe is not Germany's only. It extends to every nation, and especially to the British and American—past masters in the art of the unconscious corrupting of the minds of the masses.

that Czechs and Poles and what-not were persecuting their German minorities, to the end that, at last, the naked aggression of Nazism came to wear the guise of a struggle for freedom. Think of it! Nazism as the missionary of liberty! The wireless has convinced a nation of over 70,000,000 of the monstrous opposite of the truth.

In this frame of mind the nation has been made to believe that it is fighting a war of defence. Truth has become inaccessible. Before the German masses—and masses of other nations, too—can begin to appreciate the facts of the recent international situation, their minds must literally be born again. And that will be no boy's job. Can we make advertisement respect truth more than profit, more than propaganda? It is a problem demanding something very different from facile optimism.

Here then is something, good in itself, which has turned into a gigantic evil; which, in cold, sober reality, has made a war of total destruction easier of accomplishment.

III

There is another aspect of the modern development of war, hitherto little considered, which is even more sinister than anything which has yet happened. And this is the new possibility—the result of technology—by which a tiny minority of evil men, a mere handful, can imperil the whole of civilisation. Mr. Winston Churchill's brilliant dictum, "never was so much owed by so many to so few," carries within itself its appalling opposite, that never before was it possible for so few to damn so many.

Now that is really a paradox of human sin, that about four thousand years of historical growth and progress should land humanity back in the position it occupied, for example, in Egyptian despotism. In the Dynasty system of government in Egypt the king and his bureaucracy had it in their power to control the destiny of the entire people. That is, the few, the very few, were the absolute masters of the many. Their control of the granaries enabled them, by the simple device of starvation, to suppress all revolts. State control of the processes of wealth production, to which we are tending more and more in the world to-day, makes exactly the same thing a possibility at present. In Germany and Russia, Spain and Portugal (so-called Christian dictatorships), the possibility has been actualised. State control of the economic machine deprives all opponents of the opportunity of a job. No weapon is so effective as the threat of starvation. If liberty is to survive at all, the world has to discover some means by which economic planning (which necessitates national ownership and centralised control) is completely divorced from political power. I am not sufficient of an optimist to be sure that such means will be discovered.

The whole trend of technological evolution is to place power in the hands of the few. This fact has a sinister significance in relation to war. It completely transforms the whole problem of disarmament. In all probability it will make disarmament meaningless.

Owing to the character of modern weapons, like the tank and the bomber, a centralised bureaucracy can, in a very short time, build up a terrible striking force. Germany again is an example of this. In seven years' time, Hitler created a stronger military machine than that of Hohenzollern Germany. And all the comforting assurances of orthodox military criticism about Germany's lack of officers and inferior materials have been proved to be deluded nonsense. But compared to new developments now emerging, the tank and the bomber are almost primitive weapons of destruction. The possible uses to which, in time (and not so very long), radio-location may be put are too ghastly to contemplate. From it may come what, for a considerable time, has been the dream of science, namely, the death-ray. The problem of beam-control has already been solved. Already man can photograph by wireless. Along the same line of evolution, we shall be able to kill by wireless. The Satanic fantasy, in which the pressure of a button can destroy towns and cities thousands of miles away, will be nearing concrete achievement. This is now on the way. Experimentation in super-power, atomic disintegration, and radiation all point in that direction. The process carries further forward the tendency by which the very few can menace the many. A thousand engineers will have the power to raze towns and cities to the ground, not by the clumsy method of an invading bomber, but by the sinister silence of a stationary transmission-set.

In this situation it won't be much good talking about disarmament. What will be the point of forbidding a future possible enemy the building of warships, tanks, and bombers, if he is free to prepare the most destructive weapon of all? The only way in which a hypothetical enemy can be prevented from creating the weapon of radio-slaughter is by the forcible suppression of all technology. That is, it can't be done. Forcible disarmament, in fact, will stimulate the enemy in the other direction. This, indeed, is what happened after the last war. It was *republican* Germany, the Germany of Ebert and the social democrats, that sent its officers and scientists to *Lenin's* Russia to lay the foundation of the future Luft-waffe and Panzer divisions. The more effectively we prevent Germany, after this war, building tanks and bombers, the more intensely (probably) will German soldiers and technicians turn to the study of creating radio-weapons—in the laboratories of Britain and the United States! It will only need a few hundred of them. The international control of radio-manufacture will, in fact, be much more politically realistic than the internationalisation of air-forces. Not, of course, that that, or indeed the internationalisation of anything, will solve the problem of will-to-power. That problem calls for something which it is not within human capacity to deal with.

Since then it has become clearly possible for the few to control and imperil the many, and will become more so in the future, what guarantee can civilised society have that no minority will develop such anti-social will-to-power?

Christian realism will thus prove to be an infinitely greater factor than secular illusion for the survival of civilisation. The realisation that in human nature there is some dark principle of perversion and corruption, which operates as a dialectic of accursedness, will be a safer guide in dealing with the new problems of post-war Europe than the shallow, facile optimism of the merely humanist assumption that there is nothing radically wrong with man, that social adjustment is simply a matter of education or political power or change of international structure and relationships. Christian realism at least defines the problem. It reveals that we have to do with a dragon, not an insect. It opens the door to a new dimension in sociology, which political theorists will be wise to realise. It demonstrates the fact that, at bottom, *all our social problems are theological in character*. A very bitter pill for a secularised generation to swallow, but a very salutary one, whose purging properties will work to a bitter cleansing. To continue thinking of change in economic system or political structure as fundamental will be a flimsy defence against the demon of unredeemed human will. Economic system, political structure as the historic embodiment of man's dynamic egoism is one thing; as the source of evil, a very different thing. That has been the secular illusion which has landed Europe in the hell of totalitarian war, and the retention of which will most surely prepare a new hell of suffering and degradation—a hell which paralyses the imagination. The development of war throughout the ages, as we have studied it here, reveals an inner impotence, a radical futility, in man. Contemporary psychology tells the same story. Christian realism, to begin with, is the simple recognition of a fact.

CHAPTER III

The Testimony of Psychology and Experience

THE most startling discovery of psycho-analysis is the fact that hardly anybody is a really normal person. Just as a deeper study of war reveals that war is a normal activity among human beings, so a deeper study of the mind reveals that the average person is more or less abnormal. In other words, the human soul is a sick soul. Just as we have been mistaken in thinking that war was the exception in history, so we have been mistaken in thinking that soul-sickness is the exception among individuals. It is a general condition. We are all, to a greater or less degree, what psychology calls "abnormal." The normal is the exceptional; the abnormal is the rule.

It is interesting to note in passing that modern psychology is a vindication of the classic Biblical teaching about human nature. "For the heart of man is deceitful," said the prophet Jeremiah, "and desperately sick," which Dr. Skinner translates by the term "incurable." The radical sickness of the soul is the grand theme of the Bible. The General Confession sums it up in one sentence, perhaps the most familiar in the English language, and one that has very greatly exercised the talents for derision of modern novelists. "There is no health in us." Humanity is a diseased race. And without warning, so to speak, we find Freud in the same company as Jeremiah, St. Paul, St. Augustine, and John Calvin. He is saying one particular thing in the language of secular science which the supreme prophets and theologians of the centuries have been saying in the language of religion about the character of man: that his being is inwardly wrong; the soul itself is sick. This fact, as I have said, is merely interesting. It is not decisive. I do not belong to the school of theology which regards modern science as an authority more binding than Biblical revelation. It is simply that, on one point, science has taken a few hundred years to catch up with classic Christian theology.

The general term by which psychology indicates soul-sickness is "neurosis." The individual is "neurotic." It is a general condition of an inner conflict and mal-adaptation expressing itself in an inability to adapt oneself outwardly to society. It takes a multitude of forms ranging from simple physical disability to complex psychological disturbances like persecution-mania and schizophrenia—*i.e.*, complete dissociation of personality, so that, in effect, one is several persons having nothing to do with one another. Mr. Rom Landau suggests that that is the real trouble with Hitler.[1] It certainly was the trouble with Nijinsky, the greatest ballet-dancer of the century.[2] One of the most sinister features of modern society is the extreme neuroticism of its leading figures.

The realisation of this general neurosis or soul-sickness came through Freud's discovery of the Unconscious, the one solid unquestionable gain of psycho-analysis. It was one of the most revolutionary discoveries in the history of science; for it changed completely our understanding

---

[1] *Vide We Have Seen Evil.* (Faber and Faber, 1941.)
[2] *Vide* Romola Nijinsky's *Nijinsky.* (Gollancz, 1936.)

of the structure of the human mind. Freud came to see that what we call our conscious mind is only a small part of the total mind. The illustration usually used to picture the structure of the mind is that of an iceberg. The part below the water is very much greater than the one above the water. It was the submerged part that sank the *Titanic* in 1912. It is the submerged part of the mind that destroys human beings. Below the self-conscious processes of thought and will are profound unconscious processes, which seem to live a life of their own, independent of the control of the conscious ego. And down in these subterranean regions lie many things besides Wordsworth's intimations of God and immortality. They are not of a kind to increase man's self-respect.

Now the basic fact in man's psychic being is a permanent conflict between his unconscious and conscious self. Man is in a condition of ceaseless warfare with himself, of which social development is the embodiment. It is surely obvious nonsense to pretend that we can ever solve our social problems, so long as there exists this stage of "divided being." It is sheer infantilism to think that external adjustments can outflank this internal disturbance. It is like believing that a poultice can cure cancer. One of the most fascinating developments in psycho-analysis is the psychological analysis of political crisis and unrest, the study of how divided inner being expresses itself in political movements and events. Capitalism, Fascism, Communism are thus, partly, forms of man's permanent disease. Indeed, history itself is the fatal development which man's disease of radical self-will undergoes.

One wonders if it is an accident that both Hitler and Freud came out of the same physical environment. Both lived in pre-1914 Vienna, which was a meeting-place of scum and genius, where Western science and Eastern corruption rubbed shoulders. Hitler was acquiring the complexes whilst Freud was analysing them. But whatever may be the significance of this fact—and that it has some significance I am convinced—it is true that Nazism is the embodiment of a profound soul-sickness. Who can tell what the result for the world would have been if the Vienna art teacher had accepted, instead of rejecting, Hitler's drawings as qualifying him to become a student in the Vienna academy of art? Hitler would have painted bad pictures instead of making bad politics. Who knows? But his complete frustration, his total inability to adapt himself to society, prepared him to become the leader of an equally frustrated generation. Europe is paying a monstrous price for the divided mind of Hitler. A group of hate-crazed individuals, at a fateful juncture in European politics, gave voice to the torment of the divided mind of a whole people. Nazism is the mad fever of a sick generation.

Nazism and Fascism are but extreme instances of what is a widespread phenomenon, symptoms of an acute personal disintegration. Both Communism and the exaggerated fear of it are evidences of the same thing. This does not mean that Communism is not an objective reality, a philosophy and policy in its own independent right. It certainly is that, of course. But the influences that go to the making of Communists are, to a considerable extent, inner frustration and disintegration, for which the external social status is merely a handy peg. The proof of this lies in the fact that frequently more bourgeoisie than proletariat turn to Communism—that is, persons who have succeeded socially and economically, but have failed personally.

Whatever doubt may, quite legitimately, be entertained about this argument, less doubt is reasonably possible respecting much of the opposition to Communism. I have already alluded to the neurotic character of the Isolationists in the United States, who are exhibiting in the American scene the folly which, in Europe, went under the name of Appeasement. To say that these people are actuated merely by concern for their material possessions and status is a very inadequate interpretation of behaviour, which, from any point of view, is suicidal. It ignores the much deeper and more significant problem: namely, why it is that people feel that they have personal validity—that they are worth-while—only so long as they have material wealth or power. That is one of the greatest moral problems of our generation. Men come to identify their personal being with property. Disintegration must have gone very deep, if a man feels that he is a person only so long as he has his hands on concrete wealth. But that is, undoubtedly, the condition of great numbers of people in our society. They become crazy with fear at the very mention of the word "Bolshevism." Isolationism and Quislingism are an acute form of soul-sickness.

But neurosis reveals itself in personal relationships as well as in social and political movements. It manifests itself in the individual's purely inner being. This is especially true to-day of the sexual relationships, which, in their turn, play havoc with great political issues. It is not too much to say that the sexual sins of French politicians played a most decisive part in the final collapse of France in 1940. The acute hostility between Countess de Portes,

Reynaud's mistress, and Daladier's mistress, contributed in no small degree to the inability of Reynaud and Daladier to work together, even in the face of France's final tragedy. With the Germans less than fifty miles from Paris, Reynaud could evince a schoolboy's excitement at getting rid of Daladier from the War Cabinet.[1]

Sex has never been so explosively divisive a force in personal relationships as it is to-day. It is part and parcel of the general crisis of secular society. Marriage is ceasing to be regarded as a discipline for personal growth and integration and is becoming itself the instrument of disintegration. Men and women have, of course, always trespassed against monogamous marriage. But whereas sexual promiscuity and disloyalty used to occasion guilt-feeling, it is widely regarded to-day as natural and right. The sanctity of marriage is made to depend on the feelings of either of the partners, on what modern society calls "love," by which it ultimately means spontaneous passion. Could it depend on anything more flimsy or irrational? The loosening bonds of the marriage-tie, already a widely established fact, is a symptom of the more intense consciousness of the divided mind of man.

Amongst many other signs of the same thing—of which there is no space for discussion here—are the alarming growth of suicide during the last twenty years, and the growing number of people who are oppressed by a feeling of personal insignificance. They all point to the conclusion that so far from achieving inner unity of personality, our

[1] *Vide* particularly Elie J. Bois' *Truth on the Tragedy of France*, pp. 132 ff. (Hodder and Stoughton, 1941), and André Simon's *I Accuse* (Harrap and Co., 1941). But nearly all the literature about the fall of France deals with the political significance of the sexual affairs of French Cabinet ministers.

world, for all its boasted progress, has become more and more disintegrated, a world whose atomic individuals are increasingly at war with themselves, as well as with one another.

Freud has advanced the explanation that the multiplying discontents of civilisation are the working out of an obscure wish to die in the individual. This is a terrible contradiction in the roots of man's being. It means that the individual is being torn between two opposing forces —the will-to-live, with all its dynamic urge, and the will-to-die, with its depression of vitality. What a piece of dialectic is man! The shuttlecock of arrogance and humiliation! For ever involved in self-inflicted frustration and destruction. Mr. Lewis Mumford has suggested that Fascism is the embodiment of man's will for death. "True: the converts to fascism are themselves in some sort victims. Behind all their rabid delight in the primitive lies a desire for death: this has its expression in the devotion to war. The Brown Shirts and the Black Shirts mass to their death, shouting the name of their leader, with the same blind, fatal instinct that makes the little lemmings fling themselves by thousands into the sea, to perish there by unaccountable mass suicide."[1]

It is most significant that this revolt against life should take place in the hour of man's greatest technical conquests over Nature, when material civilisation is at the apex of its proud fame. Does it not convey to the serious mind the existence, in the very heart of man, of some profound and permanent perversity?

[1] *Faith For Living* (Secker and Warburg, 1941), p. 37.

CHAPTER IV

The Doctrine of Original Sin

THAT there is a profound and permanent perversity at the roots of the human being is the fundamental, uncompromising assertion of Christianity about human nature. To this perversity Christian theology has given the name "Original Sin"—*i.e.*, originating in man's will. The fact of radical sin constitutes the *raison d'être* of Christianity as an historic religion. Without it and without the moral impotence which is the consequence of it, without, that is to say, the fact of human powerlessness fundamentally to alter man's situation in history, the whole scheme of Christianity falls to the ground. The essence of Christianity lies in the fact that God Himself, in the person of Jesus of Nazareth, entered into history as a human being in order to do something *which man was incapable of doing*, namely, the redemption of the whole of mankind. However fantastic this may appear to the secularised mind—and I fully realise how fantastic it may seem (God as a man on two legs!)—this, in fact, is what Christianity asserts. We can lump it or like it, but there it is.

Now what could be the point of God becoming man to redeem the world, if man has the power within himself to redeem himself? Why bother in that case? *If man can solve the problem of history, the Incarnation of God in Christ becomes unintelligible and utterly irrational.* Not only does Christianity become untrue, it becomes idiotically untrue. If man can succeed in building Utopia in time, whether in A.D. 2000 or A.D. 20,000,000; if man can overcome his divided mind and re-make himself; if he can really dissipate his sense of guilt, then, of all the irrational delusions that have deceived mankind, Christianity is the most irrational delusion of them all. IF! Either man can save himself, in which case he does not need Christianity. Or he cannot, in which case Christianity becomes a human necessity if man is to be redeemed, *however fantastic it may seem*. Here is the supreme Either . . . Or. The most fateful in human existence.

Thus the doctrine of Original Sin is not a mere decoration, like a Gothic tracery. It is one of the foundation stones of the building. "And other foundation can no man lay." On it is reared humanity's only hope that its noblest dreams will ever be realised. A paradox? But Christianity is by nature paradoxical. Man's certainty of salvation rests on the certainty that he cannot look to himself for it. His hope is the hopelessness of himself. Man is like a small child with a complicated Meccano toy. You give a small child a Meccano railway set, much too complicated for it, and with the pride native to all human beings, the child will insist on trying to construct the parts into a working model. But it is too much for it. The process is too difficult for its little intelligence. If the child persists in the task, there is not a hope of success. But if it can swallow its pride and consent to its parent building it, then those separate bits of steel will become a miraculous little railway. The child's only hope of a railway is the recognition, to begin with, of its own inability to build it. Which is an analogy—imperfect like all analogies—of man's predicament in history.

The impossibility of self-redemption does not appear

to be quite so fantastic to-day as it did in the hey-day of Western civilisation, in that dim and distant golden age before the first world war. Then theologians hardly dared to mention the words "Original Sin." Was it not Sir Oliver Lodge who once said that the modern man wasn't worrying about his sins? He is certainly worrying to-day about their consequences. History has a way of rubbing man's nose into the midden he insists on ignoring. The doctrine of Original Sin seems less irrelevant to-day than a generation ago. What is really fantastic to-day is that the world should be fighting to prevent the triumph of evils which, in its shallow optimism, it had assumed to have vanished for good and all. Is it not absurd that we should look back to the ex-Kaiser as a political gentle-man? To sigh for the days of the old Prussian military caste? But the bizarre and fantastic appearance of Hit-lerism does not make it less of a fact. In the light of that, Original Sin becomes less incredible even to the proud secularised mind of to-day. Signs of this can be seen in the recent writings of C. E. M. Joad and Aldous Huxley[1]—typical children of their time.

Let us, then, briefly examine this basic Christian doc-trine in relation to history and experience.

I

The facts put before the reader in the two preceding chapters pose a profound and significant question, which demands an answer one way or another. We have seen that war is inherent in human history; that civilisation,

[1] *Vide* Mr. Joad's *Why War?* (Penguin, 1939), p. 236, his *Guide to Modern Wickedness* (Faber and Faber), and Mr. Huxley's latest novel *After Many a Summer*.

as it progresses, results in bigger and better wars. War, in other words, is a *necessary* expression of human nature with its radical egotism. Conflict to the ultimate end of slaughter and suppression is inevitable to man as he actually appears in history. To destroy his fellow is as natural for man unredeemed as it is for a bird to sing. War is not a deplorable exception, an unfortunate accident. The facts lend no support for that dangerous delusion. On the contrary, they reveal it as a basic activity of human society.

Now whatever may be our beliefs and attitudes to particular 'isms, these facts face us with an inescapable question, which all serious minds must, at least, attempt to answer. Failure to consider it would be a sign of levity and immaturity, especially in our present situation. What can be the trouble, the defect, with human nature, that war, with all its evil and horror, should be so regular and natural in its incidence? Whatever can be so wrong in man that he should make war the constant and dominant activity of history? It violates every single one of man's idealisms. Why then does he resort to it *with increasing intensity*?

This question becomes more insistent as we recall the facts revealed by psychology, which showed that, behind the outer conflict in society, there is the inner conflict in the heart and mind of the individual. The personal being of every man, woman, and child is an arena of perpetual, increasing warfare. Man is fatally divided within himself. Why? What deep disaster can have happened to personality that it should be so riven and disintegrated?

That is precisely the question which Christianity answers in the doctrine of Original Sin. History, the actual development of man in time, is the consequence of an affirmation of human will to be independent of God, Who created man free and dependent upon Himself. Man exercised the freedom with which he was endowed by God to create a new relationship between himself and his Maker, a relationship of independence; a relationship contrary to the one willed by God. History is a cosmic civil war, in which man is seeking to usurp divine prerogatives. That affirmation of independence from God is the root of all evil. It is the source of everything that is wrong in man. It is the fatal contradiction in which all history is involved and will continue to be involved, so long as man continues his original affirmation of independence, of self-subsistence. The doctrine of Original Sin is Christianity's explanation of the frustration and impotence of man in history.

But before discussing this answer at greater length, let us look for a moment at one or two non-Christian attempts to solve the contradiction of man in history.

There is first the answer given by the evolutionists, by those who have been dominated by Darwinism in its various forms, and this group includes thinkers who differ widely among themselves. But they agree in the main in saying that the contradiction in human nature is due to its animal origins. War, for example, is due to the survival of man of his animal instincts. It is the "residue" in man of his animal heritage that constitutes the defect of human nature. Pareto, who has classified these residues into six groups, is an outstanding representative of this way of thinking.[1] It is the survival in man of animal

[1] *Vide Traité de sociologie générale* (Paris), Vol. I and Chapter VI, and Vol. II, Chapter XI. Pareto was an Italian, born in Paris in a

instincts, though differently related and co-ordinated, that accounts for man's persistent irrationality.

This theory is inadequate on at least two grounds:

(*a*) It fails to account for the fact of the increasing magnitude and intensity of evil in history, as illustrated, for example, by war itself. The theory is that reason grows greater in man as time goes by, and so gradually transcends the animal. Self-consciousness increases whilst the instincts decline as *controlling forces*. If this is the case, evil and irrationality would also decrease, since they are the outcome of a decreasing animal heritage. But in fact they increase with man's expanding powers. Wheat and tares grow together, as Christ taught. It is nonsense to talk, in this case, of animal "survival." It is doing something much more effective than merely surviving. It is thriving. At what point is the animal going to begin to die? Man has now been living a civilised existence for at least six thousand years, and his animal instincts—if these are the source of his historic contradiction—are stronger than ever. When shall we celebrate the happy event of the burial of the instincts? What guarantee have we that increased applications of things which hitherto have produced negating evils to every good are going to operate differently in future?

(*b*) But this answer is also inadequate, and more seriously inadequate, on the ground that there is nothing comparable in animal instincts to evil and irrationality in human consciousness and history. There is no *sin* in the

---

year of revolution, 1848. He died in 1923. Mussolini claimed that his thinking was considerably influenced by Pareto. I can well believe it, even though the master was aghast at what his disciple made of his teaching.

animal world. Animals, for example, very rarely devour their own species. And creatures of different species can be trained to be friendly. There is, one supposes, a natural enmity between a cat and a dog. But how easily they become friends when brought up together. But the more human beings form a single society, as modern technology is so rapidly achieving, the more hostile they seem to become. This theory seems to confuse irrationality with instinct, which, as Euclid says, is absurd. Instinct is really highly rational. It is an extreme economy of function. It is the adaptation of an organism to its environment with a minimum of waste. Human irrationality is something radically different. It is the *mal-adaptation* of organism to its total environment with the maximum of waste and friction. Irrationality (and evil) is peculiarly the product of *reason* and will. Sin only enters the world on the level of consciousness and rationality. Instinct is healthy. Sex, for example, in the animal is subordinate to function. It is only in man that sex is torn from function and made central and destructive. Only in man does it become a devouring obsession—and highly civilised and rational man, to boot. Whatever the problem to which animal and savage survivals in man offer a solution, they give no answer whatever to the central problem of the basic contradiction in human nature.

Another type of non-Christian solution is the Marxist, that the evils of history are due to external social relationships. This really begs the question; for those same social relationships are themselves part of the problem. Marxism and all philosophies which look to environment, mainly, stop short of the fundamental problem. Modern psychology has settled the controversy as to whether the individual is merely a product of society or society of the individual. It is both and neither. Society is individuals in relation. But we haven't said the whole truth about the individual when we assert that he is merely in relation to other individuals. He is also in relation to a non-human order of being as well as to society, to God, his Creator. Marxism, of course, completely denies this third term, and so is compelled to make society plus Nature into an absolute. It has therefore no option but to seek for ultimate causes within the historic process, and so begs the question. It quite arbitrarily selects one element of the process—the class-struggle—and makes it the villain of the piece.

"All History is the history of class-struggle," a struggle between classes for the ownership and use of material wealth. This may be true of the history of civilisation. It certainly is not true of primitive man.[1] But whether true or not, it is the class-struggle itself, with all its contradictions, which calls for explanation. Does it mean that when the class-struggle is finally liquidated, that the basic human contradiction will then be resolved? That would be to take a very naïve view of human nature. But the Marxist psychology is very naïve.

But oftener than not, the problem is not faced at all. Facts are admitted but no ultimate conclusion is drawn. A recent example is Dr. Karl Mennenberg, an American psychologist. In a brilliant and powerful study of suicide,[2] he concludes that a scientific study of human behaviour compels us to believe that man's greatest enemy is fight-

[1] *Vide Origin and Rise of European Civilisation*, Vol. I (Oxford University Press, 1936), pp. 37-82.
[2] *Vide Man Against Himself*. (Harrap and Co., 1938.)

ing "within the lines." Man is torn by the contradiction between a will-to-power and a will-to-die. Dr. Mennenberg never once inquires what may be the cause of such an irrational paradox, but calmly proceeds on the assumption that it is within the compass of psychological science to put things right. That is to say, he refuses to face the problem. He clings more than ever to the secular illusion about man.

Another way of avoiding the problem is by making a virtue of necessity, by assuming that this condition of contradictory being is itself a good thing, a necessary condition of the good life, which, in effect, is the attitude of so searching and brilliant a social critic as Mr. Lewis Mumford.[1] He dismisses the final form of human contradiction in death, or rather converts it into a benediction. He whistles to keep up his courage. He doesn't once face the fact of the terrible defeat which death is for human personality. "Continuity for us exists, not in the individual soul as such, but in the germ plasm and the social heritage, through which we are united to all mankind and to all nature. Renewal comes through the sacrifice of the parent to the child, of the having-lived to the living and the yet-to-live. . . . Instead of being oriented, then, toward death and fixity, we are oriented to the cycle of life, with its never-ending process of birth and growth and renewal and death: a process we can neither halt nor limit by ideological fixations or cunning inventions."[2]

Mr. Mumford is here trying (in his own words) to rationalise the process of death from a frustration into a fulfilment by an "ideological fixation" of his own

[1] *Vide The Culture of Cities* (Secker and Warburg, 1940), pp. 433-40.   [2] *Ibid.*, pp. 435-8.

"cunning invention." It is in the cessation of our own being for the sake of the future that we find our deepest joy. What tragic nonsense! That may be true of the drone which, after its one act of fertilising the female, gives up its life. But man is not a drone. What can be more utterly irrational than for the individual to rejoice in cessation of being, so that future individuals may rejoice in cessation of being too? Immortality of the race, forsooth! which used to be so popular a theme in Liberal Protestant preaching. The fact of the matter is that cessation of individual being is a defeat for the race as well as the individual. Why should we try to persuade ourselves that death is anything but what it is—the final disaster and symbol of the totalitarian contradiction in which man and his entire history are involved? Why is death always a grief, even under the best circumstances; even when we are certain of resurrection? If it represents the moment of maximum joy, we should celebrate it with tambourines and laughter. But no human ideologies will ever take away the sting of death, the bitter agony of its rending. The monuments which Mr. Mumford so brilliantly derides are much more profoundly true to the tragedy of things than the shallow pretence that death is merely a biological renewal. Biological philosophy itself implies a contradiction when it dreams of the possibility of a greater prolongation of life. Mr. Bernard Shaw sees the senselessness of death, when he argues that, at the age of seventy or so, a man is only just beginning to be equipped for experience. There is more depth in the words of an old hymn:

> Show pity, Lord, for we are frail and faint.
> We just begin—and then our work is done.

Death is tragedy, frustration, contradiction.

Now this very mentality, which, apparently, has ceased to be sensitive to the existence of a contradiction, is itself a great problem. It is symptomatic of a change in the structure of the modern mind as compared with the medieval mind. Modern mind has become so inured to the idea of its own omnipotence, that it is becoming blind to the existence of anything which denies or challenges its sense of omnipotence. It has become so adapted to its self-made environment, that it has developed a protective covering against all disturbing influences, like the defensive armour acquired by primitive monsters, in the case of which the defensive armour also becomes their doom. This mentality becomes proud of its very obtuseness, and endows the conditions of its activity with non-existent qualities. The tragedy of man's predicament in history thus becomes the primary purpose of its being. Fulfilment comes to consist of loss in order to pursue a new achievement, which, as soon as it is realised, turns into its opposite, and so on for ever. The idea that the supreme joy of life lies in the maintenance, in an unbroken non-dialectic consciousness of achievement, becomes inconceivable. Life is joyful only if ecstasy is succeeded by boredom as a preparation for a new ecstasy. Unbroken ecstasy is unthinkable. The intense, unceasing ecstasy of the medieval mystics' contemplation of God is completely unintelligible to the modern secularised mind. It has lost the capacity to understand it. It can only make jokes about it. Fancy spending eternity—one of the stock puerilities this—playing a harp in heaven! This is the measure of the modern mind for things outside its experience. To it, the abysmal profundities and intensities of a St. John of the Cross are the last word in inanity.

People can become so accustomed to stupidities that ordinary common sense comes to be thought of as dangerous nonsense. For example, to our Victorian grandmothers, who never felt that they were properly clothed unless they had on three petticoats, the bare legs and minimum clothing of our contemporaries would seem a dreadful danger and a still worse obscenity. And yet is it not the merest common sense to let the sun get at your skin? A generation that had become accustomed to breathing the foul air of smoke-laden cities looked upon fresh air as a dangerous enemy. And so the very frustrations and contradictions of life, to a mind thinking only in terms of itself, have ceased to be problems. They become instead a desirable necessity. It is to this that the modern secularised mind has come. Even when its assumptions and securities are collapsing, it still does not move to a new dimension.

II

The Christian doctrine of Original Sin belongs to just such a dimension, a super-human dimension—in short, to a realm of revelation. That is, the doctrine is the formulation, by the mind of the Church, of an insight into the character of human nature which was communicated by God direct to human beings. Revelation is never a communication of doctrine, but of person and meaning. Doctrine is the systematic appropriation by a very imperfect instrument (which is what the human mind is) of the insights of persons; an attempt to correlate them to the totality of experience. In the event, the original revelation undergoes some distortion. Bergson contended that the mind is incapable of representing experience in its actual purity. The very act of thinking is an inevitable distortion. This is certainly true of revelation. Dr. Brunner has compared man's presentation of divine revelation to a gramophone recording of a great artist.[1] The recording is certainly one of the voice of the artist, but mixed up with it are things which don't belong to the original voice at all—the scratching of the needle, the overtones, the hum of the motor, etc. So the essential thing to realise in the Christian doctrine of Original Sin is that it captures and crystallises an insight into the character of human nature which the Old Testament prophets received from their communion with God. Nearly three thousand years ago, in an agricultural civilisation, men of prophetic mind and heart perceived, as in a flash, the real condition of the human heart. Jeremiah and Ezekiel, particularly, came to realise that the heart of man was corrupt; that he was doomed to self-destruction; and that the only thing that could save him from his fate was God Himself; that salvation is only of God. The *doctrine* of Original Sin is the translation of that profound prophetic insight into terms of contemporary culture.

What does the doctrine essentially assert? Three things: (a) the fact that man is God's creation in His own image; (b) that man has violated the will of God for him, which His creation of man expressed; and (c) that man's departure from God's original purpose in creation has involved him in contradiction and powerlessness, from which condition he has *to be rescued. He cannot rescue himself.* Let us very briefly discuss each of these.

(a) The creation of man in God's image.

[1] *Vide Our Faith* (Scribners, 1936), p. 10.

The doctrine, or rather myth,[1] of God's creation of man is both an imperfect and inadequate statement, because it is associated with ideas and processes in human experience which cannot conceivably correspond to anything in divine activity. The reality which the dogma of divine creation seeks to emphasise and preserve is the dependence of man's being and existence on God's will. Man comes into being as the result of God's will. He is an affirmation of the will of God. In essence. The method employed by God (which may mean nothing at all) is a question of quite secondary importance. The relation between evolutionary, biological process and self-consciousness, soul, is a very interesting speculation, but not vital. The vital point is that man and the world ultimately derive their existence from the active will of God.

Now to demand "proof," in the scientific sense, of this assertion is to ask for what is impossible and absurd. It is to imply that God's creation of man is an act similar, say, to Watt's creation of the steam-engine. Behind the demand for proof lies the assumption that the categories of science are the ultimate reality, into which all experience has to be fitted, if it wishes to attain the dignity of scientific truth. It is like asking for proof of the existence of God Himself. That is, by implication, God is put on the same level as an object, like a horse or a tree. God is

---

[1] To the average mind, myth connotes something which is not objectively true. That is not, obviously, the sense in which the word is used in this connection. I mean rather by it a statement in dramatic form of man's intuitions, which comprehends the contradictions of experience without any conscious attempt at resolving them. In intuition, man is aware of the actual existence of contradictions in his experience. The myth preserves these contradictions for thought, where doctrine, by attempting to reconcile them, tends to suppress them. Berdyaev has much that is suggestive to say about myth. *Vide* particularly his *Freedom and the Spirit*.

not an object of sense experience or any other sort of experience. He is the ground of experience—the totality of it. He is not an item or element of a process. Proof is co-ordination of elements *within* a process. God is not within a process. Similarly, to ask for proof that God created man is to assume that the divine creation of man is an element in the cosmic process, when the cosmic process is itself the consequence of an act prior to and outside it.

How then do we "know" it? The answer is—we don't "know" it, if to know means to perceive an object. We can only know it as revealed meaning, and revelation is not subject to logic, though it has its own logic. The doctrine of the divine creation is an affirmation in terms of thought of an intuition about man beyond thought.

What does the Bible mean when it says that God made man "in His own image"? It is significant to note in the Genesis narratives of creation that it is only of man that that statement is made. Man shares with everything else in those narratives the quality of creatureliness. Like the sun and moon, for example, man is made by God. About all the objects God created, Genesis says that God created each "after its kind" and saw that "it was good." But about man, and only about man, does God say: "Let us make man in our image." He distinguished between man and all other created objects. "In our own image" does state a distinction between man and all the rest of existence which is, in fact, an objective reality. There is, in fact, whether we believe in God or not, a distinction between man and every other form of matter, organic or inorganic. That uniqueness of man, says Genesis, consists in the fact, not that he was created by God—everything else was also created by God—but that he was created by God "in His own image."

What is this property or quality in the possession of which man is unique? It is the power of self-determination, of free assertion of will. It operates as self-consciousness, as awareness of individual identity. "I affirm myself." "I will. I choose." The implications of this, of course, are comprehensive and would require volumes for their adequate discussion. But the point itself is simple and fundamental. Man is aware of himself as distinct from the universe and so has the power to affirm himself.

God, in His creation of the world and man, made them dependent on His will, subject to it, man dependent as well as the rest of creation. The difference between man and the world was that man was aware of his dependence, and, by his power of self-affirmation, was able to challenge and rebel against dependence upon the Creator, *if he so willed*. Because God had endowed man with the God-like property of self-affirmation.

(*b*) Man's exercise of his independent will.

God's purpose in creation was that man should exist in a relation to Himself of self-chosen dependence upon Him; of freely-affirmed subjection to and recognition of divine supremacy, and that the rest of creation should exist in subjection to man *who was freely subject to God*. God is Lord of man, and man, under God, is lord of creation. "And God said, Let us make man in our image, after our likeness: and let them have dominion over the fish of the sea, and over the fowl of the air, and over the cattle, and over all the earth, and over every creeping thing that creepeth upon the earth. So God created man in his own image, in the image of God created he him: male and female created he them.'"[1]

Then happened something that was completely irrational, something that was the quintessence of irrationality. Which is only another way of saying that something took place which cannot be explained. Here is the ultimately insoluble problem of human existence. That something did happen is a necessary assumption, if history is to be at all intelligible, a point to which we will come in a moment. Man exercised his power of self-affirmation, not to continue the relation of subjection to God, but to rebel against it, to launch out on a career of independence of God. Man declared civil war—and has kept on declaring it ever since. Why? How? To these questions there are no answers—that is, no rational answers. The real mystery of existence is freedom, not suffering. Given freedom, given God's determination to make man free and to maintain man in the exercise of his freedom (which means God's willingness to tolerate whatever man may do in the exercise of his freedom), then suffering is no longer a *problem*. Freedom is the problem—man's power of self-affirmation. Why did God make man free? Why did He give him power to defy Himself, with all the horror and tragedy which such power involved? We don't know, and with our disintegrated mind, which is the consequence of sin, probably never shall know. Here is the ultimate blind-alley of all human thinking. The alternative to such a blind-alley at the beginning of the whole process, so to speak, is to make the entire process itself a blind-alley. At the centre of being is a maze. The alternative is to have the maze at

[1] Genesis i. 26-7.

the circumference—only to discover that the central irrationality still persists. At some point or other in human thought there is no escape whatever from irrationality. Christian theology finds it in the freedom of the created human will. That man should will himself out of his original relationship to God makes neither sense nor reason. But that is the character of sin—utter irrationality. This is the point which Dostoievsky, with his profound insight into the mystery of the human heart, grasped so well.[1] Man rebelled against God, because he wanted to. The determining factor was in his own will alone.

This raises a whole crop of secondary problems with which we cannot pretend to deal here. Did man's rebellion, which Christian theology has described by the term "Fall of man," take place in time or in a pre-mundane existence? That is, is the world as we know it, history, the result of the Fall of man? Is time itself the consequence of the Fall? These are questions involving anthropology, history and metaphysics. No statement of the doctrine of the Fall can be adequate which does not take fully into account the results of modern knowledge and research in these fields of study. But meanwhile, we are faced by this hypothesis or assumption that, at some point or other in human existence, whether in time or beyond it, man, by his own deliberate will, violated God's intention for him and the world, with the result that man, as he has appeared in history, is not man as God intended him to be when He created him "in His own image."

(c) The historic consequences of man's rebellion.

History is the record of man's re-making of himself. By refusing to be subject to God's will, man has involved

[1] *Vide Letters from the Underworld.*

himself in self-defeat and contradiction, and has literally turned God's intention upside down. Things have gone awry. War and psychic disintegration, which we studied as two examples of the contradiction of human nature, are a consequence of something radically opposed to God's will. What is this something? It is man's affirmation of himself as against God—a fact which is evidenced by the very nature of social development, by the very character of human activity. Man in history is not man as he came from the hands of God. Nothing is so striking a demonstration of this truth as man's relation to nature.

In God's intention, as Genesis states it, man was willed to be the lord of creation. But what in fact has been the relation between man and nature? It has undergone a threefold development. At first, man was the slave of nature. So far from being the lord of nature, until comparatively modern times nature was lord of man. The long era of inevitable poverty in society was conditioned by the struggle of man with nature. Primitive man had to wage a remorseless struggle for survival. His existence was one of toil and burden. With the beginnings of civilisation, with the first shaping of tools and the discovery of fire, nature became more amenable to human effort and labour. It is only within the last few generations that men have even talked of the conquest of nature. But it is only a figure of speech even now. Certainly, as a result of modern science, it is true to say that man's relation to nature has entered on a new phase, in which mankind is no longer struggling as an inferior, as a slave. Nature to-day is more subject to human will.

But the degree to which man can control nature is still very far short of a domination of nature. So long as death continues, so long has nature the final word in the struggle for supremacy. Moreover, man's temporary and partial mastery of nature through science has worked to his undoing. God's intention for man in the dominion of creation was for his enjoyment, fulfilment and development. The imperfect conquest of nature which man has now achieved through an epic struggle—it is indeed a wonderful story—does not minister to his enjoyment or fulfilment. It merely intensifies and deepens the contradiction of his situation in history. At a time when by electricity man can turn night into day, we have to black-out our cities and villages. A new abundance in wealth-production resulted in the criminal idiocy of a new kind of poverty, when, prior to the war, politics was devoted to the task of *limiting* production! The full resources of science in society are only exploited for the purpose of destruction. The greater control of nature results in greater social chaos. It is an addition to the sum total of human tragedy. This is what mankind suffers because of its attempt to live in independence of God. God's intention for man turns into its opposite.

This must be so. Along the line of independence there is absolutely no hope of anything different. Instead of all being related to the one centre, every person becomes his own centre, the result of which can only be chaos and conflict, self-destruction and futility. That is the meaning of egoism. It means that I am the centre of my own world. But my neighbour is also the centre of his world. But the world of which we are both *subjectively* the centre is *objectively* one world—not two. And two centres necessarily means a struggle for supremacy. Will-to-power never acknowledges a superior. Hence force, suppression, compulsion. The only possible way in which mankind can live in harmony and mutual fulfilment is by all men desiring the one thing—the will of God. The universal desire to do the will of God—all to be related to the one centre—would result in universal fulfilment. To become ourselves the centre results in defeat and suffering, which is what the history of the world has hitherto been.

The mode in which frustration results from radical self-will is dialectic. In other words, *dialectic is the process by which history defeats itself*. This, of course, is most emphatically not the sense in which either Hegel used the word,[1] or his deviating disciple Marx. To them both, dialectic was a beneficent process, though, curiously enough, it achieved opposite results. In Hegel, dialectic ensured the triumph of the absolute class state in Prussia. This is the best of all possible worlds, and the Prussia of Frederick is divinely ordained. It is the grandiose result of the dialectic of history. But in Marx, the same process will bring about the destruction of Hegel's greatest good, the absolute class state, and secure the triumph of the new working class. Both Hegel and Marx deified dialectic. They saw in a process, which is supremely a mechanism of self-defeat, a sign of human self-sufficiency.

But in real history, dialectic—growth through opposites—is a process of social frustration. It is a Greek word and has been so jargonised in contemporary political writing, that its meaning has been obscured. At first, dialectic was a method of argument invented by

[1] *Vide* Hegel: *Selections*. (Scribners), pp. 1-94. In Hegel's thinking the idea of dialectic took on a new meaning. It was the process by which the potential became actual by means of a development through opposites. To Hegel, dialectic was the method of God's self-expression! It meant the same thing for Marx, except that he substituted "historic process" for God.

Socrates. When any statement of opinion was made, it was challenged by its opposite. In the course of the argument between the original statement and its opposite, one was supposed to arrive at a new statement, different from both, which embodied the truth. Now what is a method of argument in logic is roughly a process in history. The whole social life of man develops through the conflict and interpenetration of opposites. An institution or system, for example, in the course of its growth, creates influences which are opposed to it. In time, these influences—ideas, new organisations, etc.—crystallise into a new institution, which is the result of the conflict between the original institution and the opposing forces to which it gives birth. An example of this process is capitalism. Wealth production for profit by means of private ownership of capital gradually creates a new working class which fights against the possessing class. Out of this conflict, socialism emerges, in which is embodied the permanent substance of capitalism and also the substance of working-class organisation.

So far from being the self-expression of God (Spirit), as Hegel taught, *dialectic is exactly the opposite, the expression of radical self-will.* It is a line of progression from confidence to failure. It is the channel in which man's intentions, as expressed in his social institutions, result in intensifying his problems, not in solving them. The facts we discovered in our study of war illustrate how it happens. The entire process may be summed up by saying: every social development of natural good in history breeds a corresponding evil which neutralises it. Democracy—a good thing surely—intensifies war. Science—also a great good—does the same thing.

Socialism—most certainly a progressive step—endangers liberty. There is no *human* good which does not also result in evil as well. Dialectic, by which the Papacy begins as a cohesive, integrating, civilising force, then becomes corrupt and destructive; by which Capitalism begins as a liberating force, releasing the energies of the individual, but ends in monopoly and suppression of the individual—this dialectic is the road on which an ego-centric humanity goes to hell. The Marxian worship of dialectic is the measure of how uncomprehending atheism can be.

This is the real predicament of man in history—that along the line of the sin of self-affirmation, man is doomed to utter futility and defeat. In that sense, the future (in different forms) will repeat the past, as our present is repeating the essence of the past. The nation-state, on a larger scale, is repeating a fundamental inability in man which the breakdown of the city-state demonstrated over two thousand years ago. To-morrow will see humanity at a higher point of the spiral of failure—a new dynamic development of self-defeat.

To this, of course, the humanist, still clinging to the secular illusion, will give an indignant denial. To-morrow, indeed, something fundamentally different will happen. *This* war will really teach mankind its lesson, etc., etc.

What is the guarantee of this fond hope?

The doctrine of Original Sin, embodying the insight of the Bible into the human heart, asserts that fallen man *cannot* now or ever break through the cycle of self-destructive futility to which his sinful pride condemns him. As far as the past is concerned, the doctrine has become a science. The facts demonstrate beyond any doubt that up to the present man has utterly failed; that he devours himself. That is a fact. Read the story, for example, in Mr. Arnold Toynbee's monumental *Study of History*—which one might describe as a study in the science of Original Sin.

But the future will not repeat the past! That is not *science*. Let that point be clear. It is a pious hope, to which the past lends no justification whatsoever. On the contrary. Over two thousand years ago, the Stoics dreamed of a world-city which men by their own love of wisdom would fashion. In the ruins of the city-state they said, "but to-morrow will be different." Alexander called for "a union of hearts," for "a joint commonwealth of Macedonians and Persians."[1] And here is mankind—2,300 years later—faced with the greatest peril in all its tragic story. By all means, let us cultivate hope—but hope in what? In the human nature which, for six thousand years, has created twenty-one civilisations and destroyed them every one? In the human nature which, at the peak of its creative powers, has reared a more gigantic monument to evil than ever before? In the human nature which, as the centuries go by, brings to perfection the possibility of universal extermination? Will humanity continue to rely on that broken reed?

There is a hope *for* man, but not *in* man. That is the first stratum in the rock of Christian realism. That is the Good News of the Christian Gospel. But it is good news only to those who have abandoned secular illusion. Christianity has no message for men whose confidence in

[1] *Vide* W. W. Tarn: *Hellenistic Civilization* (E. Arnold, 1930), p. 69.

man is unshaken. Christianity is good news to those who, first of all, digest the bad news of human helplessness. There is one way—and only one way—by which mankind can rise out of the city of self-destruction and doom to the city of redemption and healing and light. The greater the darkness descending upon man, the more brightly shines the light of the Christian Gospel.

CHAPTER V

The Only Radical Solution

THE one fundamental remedy for man's plight is that human nature shall be radically re-created, re-fashioned, so that society will be able henceforth to act, not out of the centre of self-will, but from a new centre transcending all the separated, isolated egoisms of individuals. As we have now seen, all action which arises from self-will, however good it may be in intention, is inevitably self-defeating. There is within it a principle of corruption. Therefore, if human action is to be continuously good, uninterruptedly progressive, free of the dialectic of self-frustration, it must proceed from a new source, a new will in which all men can participate. *There is no other cure for the disease of a corrupted human nature.*

As we have also seen reason to believe, this is exactly a remedy which lies beyond the capacity of human nature. Man cannot start from anything but self-will, whether in the form of naked individualism or disguised as group interest. Man—the best as well as the worst—is incapable of a complete divorce from egoism. Even during a supposed separation, furtive relations are still maintained. Humanity cannot break through the encircling fog of self-will.

But this is what God has made possible for men in the life, death and resurrection of Jesus Christ. This is the Christian Gospel, the Good News—that the prison of self-will has been opened and that mankind can escape into a new process, into a new being. In Christ man can be related to a new centre of action and life. In Him is the new root of historic, social action. What man is unable to do himself, God has achieved for him through Christ. In His life and redeeming death, there emerges into history a new humanity, whose source of action—whose centre—is not self-will, but God. This, and nothing less, is the message of the Christian faith to the world.

I

Now it is obvious, surely, that this solution of the human problem cannot be completely effective until every single human being has been incorporated in Christ, remade in His new humanity; until everybody, in the traditional language of religion, "has been saved." The stock devices and hallowed dodges for getting things done in this world are of no avail here. To abolish egoism as a source of behaviour; to act out of the supreme, all-embracing will of God means that every individual must become a new human being. An unredeemed individual means that egoism—self-frustrating conduct—is still active in society—pockets of enemy resistance in a conquered territory. To make certain, therefore, that self-will is deprived of all footing in society involves that every single person must be reintegrated in Christ. As St. John puts it: "except a man be born again, he cannot see the Kingdom of God." Every individual must himself go through the Christian experience of renewal. Majority voting is useless. We cannot legislate a new humanity. A minority of Christians cannot make society Christian. For society to become Christian—i.e., for its action to be free of self-defeat—all its members must be Christian. Passive consent will be useless. Anything less than the universal Christianisation of the world, however good or useful, will, in fact, fall short of being a *fundamental, radical* cure. And Christianity is only interested in a radical cure. Its concern with lesser remedies is all the time related to its own ultimate solution—never for their own sake. Hence, to put it in a slogan, the programme of Christianity for the world is: "everybody a Christian." This is why Christianity, in its very essence, is a missionary religion.

Everybody a Christian! From the Pope to Hitler. From Karl Barth to Mr. H. G. Wells. From the hardest-faced international financier to the softest-hearted vegetarian. From the thickest-skinned Marxist to the thinnest-skinned pacifist. From the most joyfully pessimistic believer in human corruption to the most wistful Anglican latitudinarian. Everybody a Christian!

Could anything be more appallingly unrealist, more half-wittedly Utopian? Is this not an utterly impossible fantasy? To expect to convert everybody, not to Christianity, but to become a Christian (a very different thing), is like expecting a baby to drink the whole of the Atlantic Ocean. Surely, only a crazy romantic could possibly entertain such a delusion!

Well! It certainly looks like it, especially to-day.

Even in a much more favourable situation, in early medieval Europe, when the Catholic Church of the West was all-powerful; when Europe constituted a society united at least in its values, in its accepted standards, in its recognition of Christian judgments, however little it acted on them; when the minds of men were Christian in their beliefs, in ethos, and pride was still held on a leash, even if it was a lengthy leash; when men were still aware of the brittleness of the world they lived in and had not yet developed the delusion that it was the only world they need reckon with, even in these circumstances, not everybody was Christian. Many of the highest officials of the Church were stubbornly resistant to the Gospel they preached. So if, when the social, intellectual and spiritual environment was so favourable to universal Christianisation, yet failed to realise it, how can we expect it in our world to-day? The Church is no longer all-powerful. She is only one among a host of competing institutions, breathing a hostile atmosphere. Society is no longer united in its sense of values and judgments. Considerable sections of it aggressively reject Christianity—its institutions, its theology, its ethics. More serious still, even in those who do not consciously reject, there has been fashioned a mentality inimical both to Christian understanding and behaviour—a mentality which moves in a one-world dimension, which never reckons with a reality beyond time, which is saturated with self-sufficiency, a mentality to which fundamental Christian assumptions have ceased to convey any meaning, to such an extent that classic, long-hallowed words like "atonement," "incarnation," "heaven," "repentance" have become unintelligible. "Conversion," for example, means change in the same medium—from $4\frac{1}{2}$ per cent. to $3\frac{3}{4}$. Conversion as change *from one medium to another*—as from death to life—doesn't register. If the Church failed in the green of medieval Europe, how can she succeed in the dry of modern Europe? How indeed! It is on this task of the evangelisation of our generation that the Church may break her neck. The more seriously the Church gets down to it, the more swiftly will any remaining optimism be dissipated.

Universal Christianisation, then, is not a possibility for our generation. *Nor indeed for any generation.* To expect that the entire population of the world will become Christian at any point in history is sheer utopianism. It follows, then, that social action will continue, to a greater or lesser extent, to originate from self-will in one or other of its many forms. It means, in any case, that social action, which might be conceivably Christian in its origin will, as it comes to be participated in by people not Christian, be modified or neutralised by non-Christian elements. In short, a radical cure for society is not an historic possibility. Most certainly not an immediate possibility, nor one for the near future. Society will not become Christian after the war, for instance, nor in the Europe of the coming generation.

Is this, then, merely a round-about way of implying that Christianity has no social application? Since society will not be completely Christian in history, what possible relevance can the Christian hope of a redeemed world have in our actual social situation? A very serious question. And merits, at the least, an attempt equally serious to answer it.

II

To begin with, the realisation of what the radical solution for man means, the realisation of what it involves in terms of individual, personal renewal; and, further, some understanding of what such renewal will mean for personality in terms of depth, of stress and suffering should do one thing, at any rate, which will prove to be a tremendous preliminary contribution to social salvation and health. It will redeem mankind from the curse of superficiality and the sin of self-deception. It will prevent men from nursing the easy assurance that they have banished evil when, in fact, they will have simply built a new habitation for it. In other words, the realisation of what Christianity actually is in terms of society will act as a permanent conscience in the world; as an ever-active spring of self-accusation and dissatisfaction; and consequently as a power for humility and self-knowledge. Hence, in spite of the fact that the radical solution of man's situation in history (which is what Christianity is) is not a positive historic possibility, the realisation of its meaning, of its existence as an ideal, will save society from the disaster of mistaking a superficial, temporary make-shift as the real thing. So it is plain that Christianity has an immediate negative application. It keeps the ground clear of deceptions and of the vested interests of mind and heart. It will prevent the growth of a generation which will persuade itself that its compromising of rival egoisms is the ethic of the Kingdom of God. Would that not be a precious gain?

There have been at least two occasions in the history of Europe when the mistaking of what was essentially social egoism for Christian action preceded periods of great disaster. The first was in the Europe of the eleventh to the thirteenth centuries, when the papal claims to supreme sovereignty (*plenitudo potestatis*) came to be regarded as Christian; and the second was when the technical progress and humanitarian reforms in the nineteenth century were interpreted as signs of the evolution of the Kingdom of God. Both were precursors of disaster.

In the first case, the Papacy came to insist that Europe, if it was to be really Christian, must acknowledge the temporal as well as the spiritual sovereignty of the Pope —a gigantic self-deception. In the Investiture Controversy which began in 1073, Gregory VII made claims for the Papacy which came to mean the right of the Pope to elect and depose Kings and Emperors. The established Gelasian doctrine of the Two Swords, that Pope and Emperor were sovereign in independent spheres, was revised into the claim that the Pope, "because he was the vicar of Christ,"[1] was supreme over the state. The process was prolonged. It began with Gregory VII and culminated with Boniface VIII who, in his struggle with Philip the Fair over the question of clerical taxation (in which the new force of nationalism proved stronger than Catholic internationalism), reduced to legal precision the vast vague claims of the Pope. And precisely at the time when the claims were legalised, the disintegration of Church and Pope intensified. The confusing of sub-Christian and anti-Christian action with Christian ethic preceded the colossal disaster of the break-up of the Church and European unity. The Church, before being divided and torn in the Reformation, has to suffer the shame and humiliation of "The Great Schism" and Babylonish Captivity.

In the second case, the easy optimism of Victorian England which identified "the century of progress" with the unfolding of the Kingdom of God was precursor to

[1] *Vide* A. J. Carlyle: *History of Medieval Political Theory*, Vol. I, p. 323, note 1.

the tragedy of the first world war. And after the war, the delusion that the League of Nations was a type of Christian fellowship was instrumental in leading to the second world war. This is certainly not to argue that the League was a bad thing or anti-Christian, or that it was no better than Balance of Power politics which it attempted to replace. It is simply to point out that it was not Christian, and that the superficial estimation of it as Christian was fraught with danger. The League was an unsuccessful attempt to balance the claims of rival imperialisms. That is better than war. But it is not Christian.

All through history, the self-deception that conduct is Christian when, in fact, it is not, has created a temper which aggravates the very evils it seeks to remove. It makes for self-righteousness, which is politically a source of cruelty, ungenerosity and greed. To realise that Christian social action springs from a new root, that it is a spontaneous result and not deliberately engineered, will serve to remind men, in specific historic situations, that their action is still less than Christian. It will help them to remember that, along with their opponents or enemies, they too are sinners standing under the judgment of a God who loves them both. The domination of statesmen, revolutionaries and reformers by such a temper would have made a vast difference in the Europe of the last four hundred years, especially in the Europe of the last twenty-five years. It would have meant less political persecution, for example—and less religious persecution too. It is the delusion that its system is the only true Christian system which can lead Catholic Rome still to countenance religious persecution, when it is exercised in its favour, as it does to-day in Franco's Spain.

So the fact that the application of Christianity as a positive radical solution of the problem of man is not an historic possibility should not mean its dismissal as utopian. Its negative application as a conscience in society is of great significance even for the possibility of future, sub-Christian progress. Though Christianity will not be fully realised as a social reality in this world, the contrast between it and what the world can be at any specific period will spur society to something different and better. Change is inevitable. But what the change will be is not inevitable. History is not the development of one possibility only, but an interplay of many possibilities. The acknowledgment of Christianity, though we cannot realise it, will nevertheless influence society to act on the fuller and better possibility.

But this negative relevance, so to speak, is by no means the only way in which Christianity bears on the social situation. It carries a positive application as well, which is suggested by the New Testament teaching about the Kingdom of God as being already in the world and yet to come, as both present and future. The New Testament is crystal clear in its understanding of the duality of the Kingdom. It is first of all an already realised fact. "Say not, Lo here, Lo there; the Kingdom of God is within you."[1] In this world of time and matter, the Kingdom is a going concern. Yet it is still to come. What is called, in the language of theology, the "eschatological" hope, is woven into the very texture of the New Testament. If we take away from it the expectations of the first churches of a future re-appearing of the Lord Jesus Christ, the

[1] The correct translation of the Greek is, "The Kingdom of God is among you."

New Testament would fall to pieces in our hands. The entire literature is saturated with it, from the primitive apostolic teaching in the Acts of the Apostles and Pauline epistles to the Gospel of St. John and Johannine epistles. One of the greatest contributions of New Testament criticism to a living faith is to have demonstrated that fact beyond any doubt.

The positive, constructive relation of Christianity, the one radical solution of man's historic situation, to the world is precisely through the Kingdom of God now present and active in the world. But that Kingdom is not at large in the world, like the air in space, just anywhere and everywhere. It is not, for example, present as a self-sustained identity, in the political evolution of Germany, or of the British Empire; in the growth of Capitalism or of the Socialist movement. These and similar developments are the manifestation of a humanity trying to be independent of God—in fact, the very opposite of the Kingdom of God, which, by definition, is a manifestation of a new humanity consciously subordinate to and dependent upon God. The Kingdom of God is a community of persons acting out of the will of God, not out of their own separate will. Hence, the Kingdom is concentrated in a society within a society. It is active in the world through the Church which is the only society that even pretends to initiate its action from the will of God. Strictly speaking, the Kingdom of God is not in the *world*, if by world is meant the collective humanity of self-will. It is in history, in the world's life, by virtue of the fact that the Church in which the Kingdom grows is in history, though not of it. The Church is a new society in the world, constituted of persons who consciously,

deliberately acknowledge God as King. It is the only
society in the world of which the liberal theory of the
state as "a social contract" has any semblance of truth.
"But ye are a chosen generation, a royal priesthood, an
holy nation, a peculiar people . . . being born again, not
of corruptible seed, but of incorruptible, by the word of
God which liveth and abideth for ever."[1] And whilst it is
impossible to identify the Church with the Kingdom of
God—this is the supreme Catholic heresy—the Church is
nevertheless, and in fact, the arena in the world within
which the Kingdom is present and grows. The Church is
not the Kingdom itself. Her contradictions and violations
of Christ's will are too glaring. But, in spite of all her
infidelities to Christ, she is the shell within which the
Kingdom, the new humanity, is taking shape in history
for a destiny and fulfilment beyond history.

Now the instrument for effecting the re-making of the
old humanity of self-willed independence is not isolated
individual Christians. The very idea of an isolated
Christian, that a person can be a Christian on his own,
is the myth of degenerate Protestantism; just as the idea
that the Church and the Kingdom are one is the myth of
a degenerate Catholicism. But it has become a very
popular myth in our time, which takes the form of saying
that you can be a Christian without going to church or
being associated with the Church. Which is like saying
that a man can be an Englishman on his own, without an
England. It is the existence of an England, a concrete
community with traditions and a history, which alone
makes it possible for a man to be an Englishman at all.
And so it is with the individual Christian. Without the

[1] 1 Peter ii. 9 and i. 23.

prior existence of the Christian community—the Church —no man could be a Christian. He derives his Christian being and life from Christ in the community. Without it, he would wither and decay. Without organic relation to the community, participation in its life, there can be no individual Christianity. All the talk one hears about being able to worship God in an atomic isolation from the Church is just self-deception.

Therefore, the radical re-shaping of human society is not the work of Christians in isolation, exercising a merely personal influence in corporate activities. That is the root of the fallacy that a government, for example, becomes Christian if it is composed of individual Christians. It is the same error which lies at the heart of the unbelievably shallow idea of Dr. Frank Buchman that by converting Hitler you can bring about peace in Europe. The radical solution of the human problem will not be achieved by the converting of separate individuals, and then adding them up. That idea is the disease of a merely statistical Christianity. The re-creation of mankind is more of a biological process than a mathematical one. Individuals must indeed become Christian, as we have already argued, but not as atomic, self-existing beings, but rather as cells or organs of a community.

The instrument—or agency rather—for the healing of human nature is the Kingdom of God operating in the Church. It is the effect of the impact of a new society upon an old society. It works by a process of attraction. The new society incorporates into itself the members of the old society. The Kingdom of God in the world, which is the new humanity in the making, attracts the old humanity into itself. It is not that the old humanity, the mankind of basic egoism, is going to get better and better by being individually converted, but that it will be more and more, through the Christianisation of its individual members, incorporated into a new humanity. The real struggle in the world since Christ is not between individual Christians on the one hand and individual non-Christians on the other. It is rather between a new community gradually taking shape in history, a community born not, as St. Peter puts it, "of corruptible seed but of incorruptible," and the old society, the world of natural mankind—a struggle in which the new grows at the expense of the old. Man's situation in history is already undergoing radical alteration through the passing over of the old humanity into the new.

This "passing-over" process operates when individual men and women become Christian (a point which we shall discuss in the next section), when their domination by self-will begins to be invaded by a new power, domination by the will of God. As Marx once said of Socialism, the new society is growing within the womb of the old. Within the womb of the old natural order of mankind, the society of the new order of the Kingdom of God is coming to fulfilment. Thus the radical solution of Christianity is not to be looked for in the achievements of the world as it is, but in the growth of the new society. The progress of humanity from capitalism and nationalism to economic co-operation and political federation is not in itself decisive for Christianity. This has great significance, of course, for the old humanity, for its education and discipline. But it has no significance as a sign or symptom of world-Christianisation. European federation, for example, will be a good thing, a very good thing. It will be a further dynamic development in the great historic experiment of trying to make a success of self-existent humanity. It will reveal among many other things the need for new-born men, for more and more Christianised persons. But it will not be a sign that, at last, *the world itself is becoming Christian*. It will not constitute a proof that the world is beginning to cease living out of its own radical self-affirmation; that it is abandoning its pride and beginning to live out of the will of God. A Christian society is an order of individuals in conscious subjection to God, as revealed in Christ, which society cannot become as the result of a natural evolution of institutions, but only as the result of an inner revolution, of a drastic interruption of the natural process.

What we call "ideals" are chiefly a revelation of new social needs, which existing social relations make impossible to meet or fulfil. In a profound sense these ideals (new social needs) are a progressive revelation of human inability to meet the basic demand of history and so make increasingly urgent the need for a Christianised world. European Federation, for example, is a demonstration in political form that mankind is one and should live in harmony. But the only fundamental way in which men can live in harmony is by a new revelation to God—the acceptance of His will as the source of action. But Europe hasn't got to that, so it will attempt harmonious co-operation by a forcible suppression of the native self-will of men. That is, the new demand of an emerging ideal upon the moral and spiritual resources of men will tend to make them more aware of the poverty of these resources, and so reveal the reality and relevance of Christianity. The natural evolution of social and political institutions will make clear the need for new energies and resources which can come to men only through an intervening supernatural activity. Thus social progress of the old humanity, though not itself Christian, sharpens the demand for what only Christianity can supply. An indication of this process in the present crisis of Europe is the attitude of such typically "secularised" minds as Miss Ethel Mannin and Mr. John Strachey in Britain, and Mr. Lewis Mumford (an incomparably bigger mind) in America.[1]

Now the new society (Kingdom of God) taking shape within the Church in the world will only come to fulfilment beyond this world. It will not be completed in the historic process of time and space. The problem of man *in* history will be finally solved *beyond* history. But the process of solving it is already in operation here and now. Hence, the relevance of Christianity to the whole social situation is overwhelmingly positive in character. Not only negative, in the sense that by reference to it every action or situation in history falls short of it, but positive in the sense that it initiates a process. "Revolutionaries," said Trotsky on a dramatic occasion, "must have patience." How much more must Christians have patience, who, however, can much better afford it than Marxist revolutionaries; for they are tied to time. But the Christian looks to a realm beyond time. Just as China and Russia have the vast spaces of their hinterland in

[1] Miss Mannin has been pleading for a recovery of Christian values in her *Christianity or Chaos*. It is true that she is beginning with the illusion that Christian ethics are within the compass of the natural man. Still, she has made a start. *Vide* also Mr. Strachey's *A Faith to Die For* (Gollancz, 1941) and Mr. Mumford's *Faith for Living*, in which he manages to discuss sin without once mentioning God. But it is a profound and moving book.

which to absorb military defeats, so the Christian has the vast hinterland of eternity in which history can be fulfilled.

One of the difficulties of regarding the Church as the scene of the new society is that, at first glance at any rate, the new society looks much like the old. What is still more difficult is that, as often as not, it has been worse than the old. It cannot be gainsaid that, in every age, the Church has presented a sorry example of a new society. There is no need to go over the story here. We can read the part concerning the Medieval Church in the pages of Mr. G. G. Coulton. We can read the part concerning the modern Church in the pages of Mr. and Mrs. Hammond. And we can observe for ourselves how to-day Christians are among the last to admit the abuses of the old order. All this and more is very true.

But tragic and culpable though this may be, it does not constitute an insuperable objection. That the Church remains in history the arena of the Kingdom of God is still a fact. She is still the sphere in which the new divine order is taking shape. What the record of Church history does deny is, not that the Church is the place in the world where the Kingdom comes, but that the Church is the Kingdom. To the identification of the Church with the Kingdom, history gives a conclusive and undeniable answer. But however inconsistent and unworthy may have been, and certainly has been, a great deal in the career of the Church, there is nothing in that which invalidates the claim of the Church to be the arena of God's Kingdom in history.

First of all, whilst the Church is not of the world, she is nevertheless in the world, and therefore participates in the life of the world, which opens the door to a great deal of evil and abuse. Because the Church participates in worldly institutions, as she must, she, for instance, becomes the owner of property—which is the very playground of the devil. Machiavelli once cynically remarked that a man would more easily forgive the murderer of his father than he would the thief of his property. This duality of the Church's position, with a foot in both camps, involves a great strain and tension. But the old humanity survives in the Church—a fact which the Church should never forget. Her constant awareness of it will save her from Pharisaism and pride. She, too, like the world, is a sinner—*though a different sort of sinner.*

In the second place, we have to remember that the Church is composed both of Christianised and non-Christianised people. And there is no absolutely certain test by which they can be distinguished. In any case, no human being is good enough to be judge. Only God can be that. Hence, as Christ taught, wheat and tares grow together until the harvest—which will not be garnered in history. The false thrive along with the genuine, but it is only God who sees the hearts of men. It is only He who knows all that is in a position to judge who is Christian or who is not. So always the Church has within her ranks un-Christianised souls. And even the Christianised souls are only imperfectly so. The fact that the Church survives such a handicap and continues to be a living reality is evidence in favour of her claim.

In the third place, we must recognise the fact of the permanence of the Church in her different forms, and that she alone gives an example of action which is not subject to the law of dialectic. The Church changes, but never into the opposite. Always there is within her the amazing power of renewal, of recovery. The Roman Church survived the decay of her Holy Roman imperial contemporary. She survived the terrible wounds of the Great Schism and the Reformation. The oldest institution in England to-day is the Church, essentially the same through all the changes. The Church of England worships the same God, acknowledges the same Lord, celebrates the same redeeming death, and looks to the same hope to-day as she did a thousand years ago. The only place in our world to-day where a Christian citizen of the Roman Empire of the second or third century would feel at home would be the Church. In every other institution he would be completely at a loss. Democracy—Capitalism —Socialism—Fascism? These would mean nothing to him. But in a church service, his heart would kindle. "I believe in God the Father Almighty, Maker of Heaven and Earth, and in Jesus Christ, His only Son, our Lord, who was conceived by the Holy Ghost, born of the Virgin Mary, suffered under Pontius Pilate, was crucified, dead and buried. He descended into hell. The third day He rose again. . . . I believe in the Holy Ghost, the Holy Catholic Church. . . ." The very same words he used to recite in Rome or Antioch or Alexandria or Athens or Corinth so long, long ago. While, therefore, there is enough and more than enough to deny the claim that the Church itself is the new society, there is also enough and more than enough in her record to confirm the great truth that it is within her being and life that the Kingdom operates in the world. This fact makes Christianity doubly relevant to man's historic situation.

III

The supreme necessity then in the present situation, and in every other situation, is that individual men and women should become Christian, which is more easily said than done. This is more important for the ultimate fate of mankind than military victory even over Hitlerism; more important than to construct the new social and political system. Not, of course, that these are alternatives. Europe will fashion some new kind of working international relationship, whether men become Christian or not. The world never stands still nor remains the same. Being a dynamic creature, man will invent new social structures. This will happen anyhow. But the new structure, like all the others, will prove to be temporary. Like all the others it will contain within itself the seeds of its own destruction. The new order in Europe will be another makeshift solution of man's problem. In no sense will it be a radical solution. Of course, it is important that Europe should discover the best makeshift which is historically possible. European federation of independent sovereign states will be infinitely better than German hegemony. A regional organisation of Europe would be still better than federation of sovereignties. All this is of great importance, and the Church should do all in her power to bring about the best possible. But when all that is realised, the best possible will still be only second-best. It will not be either a radical solution or the beginning of a radical solution.

But the Christianisation of individuals will be a process of radical solution. And that is why it is of infinitely greater importance than any second-best procedures.

More and more the Church should judge all social changes in their relation to the Christianisation of individual persons. What are the social changes and developments which will most encourage the Christianisation of the individual? That is the true attitude for the Church in social questions. That is only another way of saying that civilisation exists for the sake of religion. Mr. Arnold Toynbee has said that his own attitude on that question has undergone a revolutionary change.[1] He began by thinking that religion was the enemy of civilisation; then he came to think that religion was the servant of civilisation (which was good Liberal Protestantism). Finally he has become convinced that civilisation exists *for the sake of religion*. Further development calls more and more for Christianised persons. Nothing is so important for mankind.

What, then, does "Christianisation of the individual" mean, and how can it be achieved? This question is indeed the crux of the whole matter.

The first, fundamental and absolutely indispensable condition, without which it is for ever impossible for any man to become a Christian, is (*a*) that he should realise that the supremacy of his own will is the root of all sin against God, and (*b*) that he should desire, with his whole being, to abandon that supremacy in favour of the supremacy of the will of God as the new source of life and being. *About this there can be no argument.* No discussion of terms. For the man who would become Christian, it is not a matter of negotiating an armistice. It is unconditional surrender. There can be no parley

[1] *Vide* his Burge Memorial Lecture, "Christianity and Civilisation" (S.C.M., 1940).

whatsoever on the question of self-will. It has to be
abolished lock, stock, and barrel, man-behind-the-gun-
and-all. "There is no other way . . . but to trust and
OBEY." That radical ego must be dethroned and no
questions asked. As we have seen in the preceding discussion, the radical ego is the prime source of man's
disaster in the world; the soil out of which grow all the
tragedies, evils, and irrationalities of history. Therefore,
the realisation of its totalitarian evil is a necessary pre-
cedent to the desire for its abandonment. The dissipation
of egoism is going to be a terrible, tearing, tormenting
process. How can man treat as a joy-ride the process of
undoing Original Sin in his heart, mind, and will? Without a profound ever-present conviction, which ceaselessly
pricks and burns, it cannot even be begun. And most
certainly can never be persevered with. That is where we
begin.

And this is what the New Testament means by repentance. "Except ye repent and be born again, ye can in no
wise enter the Kingdom of Heaven." Repentance which,
in the New Testament, is the gateway to salvation is not
a mere feeling of sorrow or contrition for a mere act of
wrongdoing. The sorrow or regret I feel when I act
impatiently or speak angrily, for instance, is not repentance. At least, it is not what the New Testament
means by repentance. That sort of feeling, very often,
fosters our basic egoism by making us think that down at
bottom we are not so bad as that particular action would
seem to indicate. Contrition, without repentance, is a
feeder of pride. Repentance is not contrition for any
action, or for anything that we *do*. Repentance is contrition for what we *are* in our fundamental nature and

being. With such a realisation of heart, mind, and will, contrition for separate acts becomes a source of humility, because it will remind us of what we are in our essential self. What is radically wrong with all of us is not that we perform more or less frequent acts of wrongdoing, but that we are wrong in our deepest roots. We are all-pervasively self-willed. We live of ourselves and not of God. Repentance is the realisation that that is our condition.

It is important that we should understand that repentance is an activity of the whole personality. Christian teaching has tended to present repentance as primarily an emotional activity, a state of feeling, of which regret, sorrow or contrition is the chief characteristic. But this state of feeling, strictly speaking, is a consequence. Repentance is also a rational, or rather, intellectual activity. It is an operation of the mind, an effort at understanding. It is that activity by means of which we come to say, "I see." Repentance also is an exercise of will. It is volitional. Unless I will to become different, the mind will not follow. Thus there can be no repentance without the participation of the whole personality. It involves belief, conduct, and emotion, to which correspond theology, ritual, and prayer. There can be no abandonment of self-will if one believes, for example, that human nature is fundamentally right and sound. Nor if the intellectual conviction does not produce a longing of the heart. There can be no abandonment of self if the longing produced by the intellectual realisation does not spur the individual to do something about it, as we say. Repentance is personality in a state of intense concentration.

How can men be brought to this experience?

It is when we confront such a problem as this that we can see the utter stupidity of the idea that men can be Christian or become Christian in isolation. When we ask ourselves how men and women can be brought to repent, we shall see quickly enough the need for the Church. Without her it is concretely impossible for men to come to repentance. In theory, there is nothing impossible in people experiencing repentance in isolation from the Church—especially in mere modernist theory. In the abstract, I suppose, it is quite possible for the man to whom Sunday, for example, is an opportunity to motor to country or seaside (to refresh the weary titan, etc.) to be stricken dumb with realisation. In the abstract, the Brighton road can become another road to Damascus.[1] In the abstract. But not in the concrete world of hard reality. Things do not happen in that way. In the actual world of men and women, of tradition and history, of multiple influences, men come to the threshold of Christian experience only in the Church, in the community which God has specially founded to be the organ of the Kingdom of God in history. So the first answer to our question how to bring people to repentance lies in the necessity of bringing them into living association with the Church. In the Church, with her corporate life, her preaching and teaching, her sacraments and worship, her demands and obligations, her world-wide responsibilities; it is here that men may become aware of the Holy Ghost, without the co-operation of whom there can be no

[1] In these days, when the Bible has become a closed book to so many, the allusion to Damascus may be missed. It was on the road to Damascus, though not in a motor-car, that Saul of Tarsus experienced repentance and was afterwards known as Paul.

repentance, however clearly men may realise and long for change.

It is in the Church that people can be taught the beliefs necessary for repentance. And belief is necessary. There will be no repentance without a theology. Let that be crystal clear. Let the literary amateurs understand, who have yet to learn the A B C of Christianity, to the values of which they are now saying we must return, that theology is not a perverse, vested interest of professionals, but an absolutely fundamental necessity. These famous "values" of Christianity are dependent on theology. The idea that Christian values can be recovered for modern civilisation without a theological revolution is the dream of ignoramuses. Theology is one of the foundation-stones of repentance. For example, how can a man repent, in the New Testament sense, without a belief, not merely in *a* God, but in the *personal* God and Father of Jesus Christ? How can a man repent without the belief (implied at the very least) that that God is his creator and sovereign? And these two beliefs—that God is Personal and Loving, that He is creator and sovereign —involve the whole of the Biblical Revelation. Only in the Church can man learn these truths necessary unto repentance.

In the Church, too, can men be trained in the discipline necessary for repentance—and only in the Church. And without discipline repentance is impossible. The transition from the natural humanity of self-will to the new humanity in Christ is not going to be a joy-ride. Repentance is not a pleasure. It goes against the grain. Transitions are always a difficult process. That is their nature. Even transitions from one phase to another within the old order are immensely difficult and painful. Birth is synonymous with pain. In social, historic development, transition is only another name for revolution. And revolutions are notoriously a costly and bloody business. And that, let it be repeated, for change from one form of the old to another form of the old. But what about a transition from the old to the New, the literal, unique New? That too is a matter of blood. "For without the shedding of blood there is no remission of sins." But real repentance of the person from the natural to the spiritual man is more difficult than revolution. The proof of this apparently fantastic statement is that the world prefers revolution to repentance. So repentance involves a discipline—the discipline of confession and prayer. And where, but in the Church, can that discipline be acquired?

In the Church, finally, and only in the Church, can men enjoy the fellowship and co-operation necessary for repentance. Men cannot repent on their own. Repentance, though *personal*, is essentially a social process. And first, and supremely, repentance needs the co-operation of the Holy Spirit. Over and above all that the Church may do as a corporate organisation, the Spirit must be active. Without the Spirit, the dry bones shall not live. Baptism —Confirmation—Holy Communion: these are the channels through which the Spirit comes to the individual. Frequently, alas! these remain empty channels. But—in these activities of the Church, the individual is never quite safe and secure from the impact of the Holy Spirit. The person partaking of the Bread and Wine runs every time the risk of being gripped by the Holy Ghost—and then only God knows what may happen.

Without the presence of the Spirit in the intellectual, volitional, and emotional processes of the individual, these do not finally add up to repentance. The Barthian school has emphasised the work of the Spirit in repentance to such an extent as to make it appear that the individual has nothing to do with it. But the Barthian over-emphasis was a reaction to the humanist delusion of human omnipotence, when God played second fiddle to man's first. And like all reactions, it went too far. If repentance is entirely and only the work of God, then man is a mere automaton. And that is heresy. But neither is repentance entirely the work of man. That also is heresy—a heresy which has peculiarly cursed modern Christianity. It is a fact that it sometimes happens that men learn at last the nature of self-will and desire to become different—and yet nothing happens. The processes do not fuse into repentance in any recognisable sense, the only explanation of which would seem to be that the Spirit is not present. The Spirit must co-operate if there is to be genuine repentance. "Likewise the Spirit also helpeth our infirmities."[1] The Church is the arena of the Spirit's historic movement. Thus, repentance for this generation, especially, is primarily a question of re-association with the Church.

Of course I do not for a moment pretend that this is a complete answer to the question, or even, in one sense, that it is an answer at all. I have not attempted any systematic discussion of what is involved in repentance. What I have tried to do is something much less ambitious, namely, to indicate the concretely necessary condition in which the men and women of to-day may be in the

[1] Romans viii. 26.

position to come to repentance. What that condition is admits of no doubt whatever. It is that the Church should become for this generation what it once was for previous generations—a dominating institution and power. In other words, religion must recover its priority in the mind of our time. The failures, the inadequacies and grave imperfection of the Church do not affect this necessity at all. I am well aware of the defects of the Church. As a priest in the ministry of the Church, I may be more acutely aware of these defects than any external critic. The defects are appalling, God knows. But they do not alter one fact, at any rate: *that with all her defects, she is still the only institution which stands in the world to-day for the proclamation that the one radical cure for men in history is the new re-created humanity of Christ's redeeming Cross and Resurrection.* And it is only within her historic life that men can be orientated towards repentance, which is the first step in the radical solution of man's problem.

How, then, can our generation be made Church-conscious? How indeed! When I ask myself that question, I feel as the prophet Jeremiah must have felt when he said, "I am but a child." I have no ready-made, cut-and-dried, cure-all scheme. Neither have I confidence in any such schemes. So many of the discussions and proposals for the evangelisation of our generation seem to me to be lacking in appreciation of the colossal depth and difficulty of the task—prescribing pills for earthquakes. But one thing seems to be certain: there can be no recovery of Church-consciousness unless men come to feel (and to feel rather than think, which means that a lot of thinking must be done as a preliminary) that the

Church is somehow relevant to the whole immediate situation of Europe and the world. This does not mean that men will necessarily become Church-conscious, even though they do come to feel that the Church is a relevant reality, and not a mere historic decoration or survival. But without it, it is quite certain there will be no revival of Church-consciousness in our time. In the final chapter, therefore, we shall examine the question how Christian realism bears upon our immediate situation.

CHAPTER VI

The Immediate Relevance of Christian Realism

I

ONE possible reaction of readers to our conclusion that Utopia is not realisable in this world, that every new social order, be it socialist or democratic, will also in time produce its negating opposite—to all this readers may react by saying: "In that case, what's the good of doing anything at all? Why trouble ourselves? If it is certain that, after all the terrors and tragedies of this war, the new European order will prove not to be permanent, but be the breeding-ground of new conflicts (though not necessarily military ones), why not let things take their own course? Why not every man for himself, and the devil take the hindmost?" In other words, since the Christian solution, which involves everybody becoming Christian, is not a realist possibility here and now, what possible bearing can Christianity have upon our immediate problems? What relation can a religion concerned with ultimate, super-historical destiny have to civilisation here in history? Can a religion whose hope for man is Heaven be any guide to man on earth? This, or something like this, is what many readers will doubtless ask. The question does not arise *logically*. Since, however, none of us is really logical, the question forces itself upon us in spite of logic, and must be answered.

95

There is also another consideration which makes it necessary to reply to this objection, and that is that the majority of people to-day do not believe in any destiny for man beyond this world. It doesn't count in their scheme of life or thinking at all. To them destiny is of this world, and of this world only. Also, to many of those who *think* they believe in a world beyond this, their belief is a very thin, ghostly affair. It doesn't fundamentally influence their thinking and conduct. The number of people in modern society to whom Heaven (a super-historic order of reality) really exists and counts is a very tiny minority—a fact which, incidentally, demonstrates the profound and disastrous difference between the modern soul and the medieval. Hence, if our world is to recover Christianity, it is an absolute necessity that it should become convinced that Christianity is relevant and necessary to our immediate situation; to this Europe with its war crisis, its tangle of hates and contradictions, its neuroses and frustrations, and its gigantic post-war problems. And in a profound sense, this is a right and proper instinct; for alone among the great historic religions, Christianity realises the vital significance of history. It alone is aware of the tension of time and eternity. It is the only other-worldly religion in which this world is of *decisive* significance, in which Heaven is organically related to earth. This question, while it manifests a tragic anti-Christian scepticism, does, at the same time, involve the very essence of Christian faith. Christianity does not simply hand over the world to the devil. It insists on making it a very important part in the process of divine providence. Let us then "go to it."

The fundamental *social* fact of our time is that we are

witnessing the end of an age, of an epoch. The era that was ushered in with the Renaissance, with the Reformation and the rise of Capitalism, is passing away in the upheavals of world-war (two in a single generation), civil wars (at least five major ones in twenty years), permanent social conflict, and the emergence of a series of political and economic problems impossible of solution within the framework of the disintegrating capitalist order. This is no longer a matter for argument or doubt. The world has been debating this question for nearly a hundred years, at least since the Communist Manifesto in 1848. And now the conclusion is becoming too insistent for further denial. History has taken the argument away from the theorists into its own brutal hands. It is underlining the collapse of modern capitalist Europe in gory red, which is history's favourite colour. The continued denial of this fact is no longer a rational act. At the risk of seeming to be dogmatic—a risk I cheerfully run—I will say that to persist in denying this Mount Everest of a fact (collapse of modern capitalist Europe) is evidence of disease of mind, of a deep neurosis. Even the most wicked of social reactions and counter-revolutions, namely, Nazism and Fascism, is bound to take the form of revolution and social progress. Its only possibility of mass-appeal lay in its promise of something new, something future and untried. Hitler's European New Order, and let us make no mistake about this, is a violent solution for a social state of things which could no longer continue: the effort to operate international, world-wide economic forces within the outworn framework of class and national sovereign states. The unification of Europe as a single productive and political unit under German control is *a* solution, a devilish solution it is true, yet a solution, of the intolerable higgledy-piggledy of twenty-four sovereign states each trying to subordinate a universal social process to local, provincial ends. Hitlerism is the consequence on the social level of Europe's failure to keep its appointment with history, of its refusal to adapt its economic and political structure to the new dynamic needs of society as they arise. Even Fascists recognise that existing capitalist Europe is dying. To have *less* insight than Fascists is, surely, conclusive evidence of spiritual blindness and mental paralysis. To try to play any longer the part of Procrustes in our world is an activity of the politically demented.[1] Sheltering under The Umbrella!

Now whether the Marxist contention is true or not, namely, that ideas are a product of productive and social relations, there can be no doubt that modern Europe could not have developed to its present point without the secularised mentality; without, that is, the assumption of the self-sufficiency of man; without the gradual domination of the idea that man's destiny can be realised in this world; without the idea that the needs of man's total being are capable of being satisfied by human society alone. This is a point of vast and fundamental significance, and must, therefore, be so emphasised, that it takes root in the mind of the reader. The very possibility of a better order than Capitalism depends upon the realisation of this fact. If the Europe of the post-war era is to provide hope and stimulus for living to the common man, this profound fact must be grasped.

[1] Procrustes was an ancient Greek innkeeper who, when his guests proved to be longer than his beds, used to employ the charming method of cutting off their legs to make them fit the beds! He was the ancestor of the contemporary die-hard and last-ditcher.

Max Weber in his *Protestant Ethic and Capitalism*[1] argued that Capitalism was the result of this mentality, with its corollary that men were primarily isolated, atomic beings, and that society was simply the sum total of individuals. Marx argued that the whole range of ideas characteristic of Capitalist society was the result of developing class relations. Neither argument is true in the extreme form in which Weber and Marx present it. The fact probably is that what happened was a synthesis of both. The new Renaissance idea of this-worldliness initiated the modern order, which in the course of its development intensified it. It is certain, however, that our modern civilisation is the native, necessary expression of the view that in this world men can enjoy complete happiness, security, and fulfilment, that it is within the power of society, through increasing wealth consumption, education, leisure, and organisation, to create the instrument for achieving this end. Our civilisation is the working out of that idea in social, political, economic, and cultural institutions.

Now this view of the world as man's home and native heath had two consequences in terms of thought and morality which have proved to be disastrous. First, there developed a political theory (the complete opposite of medievalism) of man as an atomic separate individual, and that the function of state and society was merely to protect the individual *as a separate atomic being*. The individual, as such, has certain inalienable fundamental rights in himself. Society's job is to protect the individual

[1] In a slightly modified form, Mr. R. H. Tawney has used the same argument in his *Religion and the Rise of Capitalism*, which is now obtainable in the Pelican series.

in the exercise of those rights. In so far as it is possible to say that any theory has a beginning, we may trace the rise of this view to Marsilio of Padua (1324). It reached its classic statement in Hobbes and Locke. By the time of Locke, the inalienable individual right had crystallised into the right of property. So in practice, the protection of individual rights by the state came to mean protection of the right of the strong to exploit the weak. The reaction against this theory began with Rousseau, whose doctrine of a General Will has finally come to full flower in Hitlerism. Hitler claims that he is the mouthpiece of the German General Will, the Volk. There is more truth in his claim than the political Left Wing cares to admit. Nazism is the twisted, crazy protest of a tormented community against the outrageous capitalist theory of man as a mere atomic individual. It goes to the extreme of saying that the tribe is everything and the individual nothing.

The second consequence is the evaluation of life in purely material terms. The only reality in politics came to be power. The only reality in personal and social life was money. Whereas the characteristic institution of medieval Europe was the Church, the characteristic institution of modern Europe has been the bank. The banker is the real priest of modern society, complete with his holy mysteries of credit and money-market. Machiavelli was the philosopher of power-politics, and Adam Smith the philosopher of capitalist wealth, with Von Mises as the philosopher of the money-market. From this illusion about the character of this world of time and matter as an arena of complete security and achievement for mankind, with its twin pillars of man as a separate, self-contained individual for whose protection society exists, and money as the concrete end of human striving —from this devil's brew have been concocted the horrors and enormities which we now know to be inseparable from our capitalist civilisation.

And here we come to the root of the whole matter: if Europe and the world—for Europe now has come to mean world—are to build a new order, as distinct from a merely other order, a basically different social order; if Europe is to create a whole series of different social and political and economic institutions; if, to specify, men are to be saved from poverty and recurrent war, from the running sore of acute class conflict, with its periodic phases of chaos and crises, *then the secularised mentality of modern man has to be changed*. As regards the basic change necessary for a new order, Christianity has more political and social realism in its little finger than current humanism (Left or Right) has in its entire make-up. How can you institute *and subsequently maintain* an organisation of society for a scheme of purposes, of aims and objects, with the mentality and attitudes which have fostered and been fostered by a completely contradictory scheme of purposes, aims, and objects? That is a conundrum compared to which squaring the circle is as easy as winking. The answer is very brief and simple: you can't! It is utterly impossible to fashion a co-operative European order with minds and hearts that have been moulded and shaped by (*a*) the idea that man is a self-contained individual with rights of his own apart from society, and (*b*) the idea that those rights find their supreme, essential realisation in the pursuit of material gain in power or money or both. It will be like trying to play a symphony with a kettledrum, or writing a poem with a bayonet. Among Europe's 400,000,000 population there are masses and masses of people (in *all* classes, bourgeois as well as working-class) who think and feel in their bones that the good life lies in maximum acquisition and consumption of things and that the societies in which they live exist merely to provide them with the opportunity to do that. They are rebelling against society because of its failure to provide them with the opportunity. If they continue to think and feel in that way, then we shall proceed to try to create another social order to attempt the same thing. *And that means chaos.* If society is artificially continued as an endeavour to provide a mob of separate individuals with material wealth to live in their individual self-sufficiency, Europe will be taking a short-cut "as the crow flies" to a new jungle, compared with which the jungle known to anthropologists will be a Garden of Eden.

There must be a new and different social order in which the technological dream of a tropical abundance of things for a rabble of isolated units is replaced by a different sort of ideal altogether. It must be a society in which individuals only find rights in social relationship, to whom society is not a fat-uddered cow to be milked *ad lib.*, but as the arena and instrument of a personal, spiritual development. So we find ourselves in the position of having to reverse gear, of finding our way back to the high-road of European development, back from the side-road which Europe has been travelling the last four hundred years. This does not mean back to medieval feudalism, to institutions that history has finished with. Let octogenarians enjoy such lunatic luxuries. But we've got to find our way back to a different spirit, to a different vision of man and society, to a different understanding and appreciation of the nature and character of this world. If the modern era proves one thing certain beyond all others, it is this: it is an impossibility to make society an instrument of material aggrandisement for isolated, self-contained individuals. For man is not an isolated individual. He is a personal, social being. The delusion that he is self-contained had become so unbearable that rather than continue with it, a great deal of Europe went Fascist—*i.e.*, men at last refused to be individual on such terms and lost their identity in the tribal national mass. Others, more fastidious, like Mr. Aldous Huxley and Mr. Gerald Heard, tried to lose it in a modern form of Buddhism.

How can we build the new society of persons with minds that have become de-personalised, secularised, and isolated? Or, worse still, with minds that have escaped from the burden of individual identity into a tribal warren?

It is obvious, then, that not merely have we to change our ideas, but that we must bring to bear on our problems minds and hearts that have been saturated and re-shaped by different ideas and ideals. A new process of thinking and feeling must be initiated in the individual, as a result of which the ideas of man and society and the world and of the ends of living generated by modern European capitalism will loosen their hold. And here we come to another rock-bottom necessity.

The modern ideas of man as an atomic unit and of money as the symbol of the aim of living did not drop out of the blue. They arose out of a new development of self-will. They are the product of the fatal miscalculation about the nature of the world and the capacity of man. It may be difficult if not impossible to trace the inner, logical connexion of these ideas. But it is a fact of history that the modern ideas about man's relation to society and the embodiment of it in a frenzied pursuit of wealth to the subordination of all else became dominating influences in civilisation only after the assumption about this world as man's destiny had taken root. It is a fact that absolute political power in medieval Europe was severely restrained. It is a fact that the Catholic doctrines about usury and the Just Price prevented the pursuit of material gain from seizing the reins of civilisation. Medieval Europe looked on the business-man with a less kindly, awestruck eye than does modern society. If it is difficult to see the logical connexion, it is not so difficult to see the moral connexion between these ideas. Once assume that man has to find his destiny, his fulfilment in this world, then this world becomes an obsession. And the deeper that assumption penetrates a man's mind and being, the more all-absorbing and important this world becomes. What is this world but the tangible, concrete material life? If this world be all, then exploit all its resources and possibilities. In due course this takes shape as the worship of things.

The creation of a new order in Europe demands a new view of man and society and the purpose of social organisation. How can we engender these new ideas, if we persist with the fundamental delusion about the nature and possibility of earthly existence? To continue in the belief that this world is man's true destiny is inevitably to continue with the characteristic modern ideas of man, society, and life, *whatever new disguise they may wear*. And, of course, they will assume new disguises which will deceive many, both in the Church and out. Ideas, like everything else human, have to change in order to remain the same.

The future of Europe depends, then, upon the inculcation in the minds of our generation of a new mentality, of an attitude which does not make man the prisoner of time and matter. This mentality can only be created by the conviction that being and existence are not confined to this world only; that man is a citizen of two worlds. Such a belief about man and his destiny will have more power to dethrone materialism than anything else. And that, in a word, is the gist of Europe's immediate problem. How to deflate and destroy materialism? How to induce in men an attitude of heart and mind of such a quality that material pursuits and rewards will lose their fascination and magnetic power? What appeal, for example, could Hitler have exercised on a France whose leaders, at least, had been uninfluenced by self and power? Suppose the little butcher boy of Chateldon (Laval) had become a saint—a real saint with his roots in a world other than his native Auvergne? Hitler would have appealed in vain. That is Europe's most significant and urgent problem— the creation of individual men and women to whom society is not a racket of selfish gain. Not, to begin with, individuals who have the right ideas of the progressive societies about European federation, sex emancipation, education, etc., but individuals whom things, mere things in whatever form, are powerless to bewitch. It is such people as these who can make new social institutions, which look to new values and purposes, really work.

Right ideas by all means. I am in favour of right ideas, especially of those which I happen to think right. But first the new mentality, the heart in which this world is not the only reality.

This new mentality is the raw material of a new order, of a better experiment in civilisation; of a civilisation whose defects and failures even may prove to be more potent in the spiritual discipline of the world to its redemption in Christ; a civilisation whose successes, still falling short of Christianity, may bring the world to a better appreciation of what Christian society could mean. Such a new order is a concrete, historic possibility here and now. The technical conditions for such an order have been achieved and that is a tremendous epic feat of human skill, courage, and invincibility. Mankind, which has been eternally one in God, is now physically one in labour-processes, even though it has become more socially and politically divided than ever. But the technical, objective conditions for a new degree of subjective, social unity undoubtedly exist. Their fuller exploitation only awaits a new spirit. The technical possibility for a new chapter in history has emerged into reality. It is the moral condition which is lacking. And that can be best described by saying that it is a different conception of society and of the ends which society should serve. No such different conception can possibly come from a mentality that is imprisoned within the dimensions of this world only. So new mentality.

II

And this is the grand relevance of Christianity to our immediate situation; this is where "pie in the sky" has something to say to to-morrow's dinner here on earth. And this is the greatest contribution the Church can give to mankind in its present difficulties.

Now whatever criticism may be made of the Church, it cannot be said that she is a completely this-worldly institution, though she has frequently tended to become that. But the religion she witnesses to in history being, in essence, an other-worldly religion, has made it impossible for the Church ever to succeed in becoming completely this-worldly. However dense be the obscuring fogs, there always peeps forth from her "the light that never was on sea or land." This indeed has been the greatest quarrel of a secularised age with the Church. It has been the text of the juiciest jibes at her expense. But the stone that was rejected by the builders of Utopia has, in the anguish that has overtaken Europe, become the head of the corner. It is precisely the other-worldly element in the Church's worship and theology that has now become the thing of greatest immediate social significance, the thing of greatest potentiality for social renewal. It is the conviction that man's true destiny lies in another world that can be the most powerful dissolvent of Capitalist materialism, of the idea, too, that society is a medium of individual aggrandisement. Let the Church "be fruitful and multiply" the number of men and women in society to whom another world becomes a reality to be reckoned with, and she will let loose in the world a new creative social force. This social force is not one of the automatic by-products of Marx's famous productive relations. It is rather the by-product of a new relation between man and God.

It is in the engendering of this conviction that the

Church can render a unique service to civilisation. In this field she has no competitor. In the devising of plans, schemes, and devices for new social organisation, she has numerous competitors who are much better equipped. Diocesan conferences, episcopal retreats, and church assemblies are not the best means for deciding on questions like political federation, new forms of wealth distribution, international armaments, access to raw materials, etc. Let churchmen do some thinking on these questions, indeed a lot more thinking than they have done up to the present. Let the clergy especially bestir themselves on the vast complex of new economic and social problems, if only to discover that these problems, in the final analysis, *are theological in character*. Let the politicians dwell a bit more on theological questions, so that they may discover that they are political in character. But what the Church can do, as a society, is something which no other organisation is even thinking of; something which must be done if the dominating ideas, which have brought Europe to disaster, are to be dethroned. And that something is to recall in the minds of this generation the forgotten fact that men are creatures of eternity as well as of time. Here is the immediate relevance of Christian realism.

A minority of men with this realisation in the roots of their being have in them the power to launch civilisation on a new career, in which the common man and his wife and children, plain John Smith and Mrs. Smith and the kids, can look forward with renewed hope. What a nightmare the last twenty years have been in Europe! A friend of mine, principal of a theological college, has been wondering whether it would not be a complete waste to send his son to Oxford to be educated in the humanities, in a world which clamours more for mechanics than for culture. But culture can have a new birth, if there are sufficient men and women in the world who understand that its fulfilment lies in another realm. Where can we find these men and women? It is certain that if they will not be found in the Church, they will not be discovered anywhere else.

In A.D. 410, Alaric the Goth, one of the predecessors of Hitler, conquered Rome. It was the beginning of the end of the Roman Empire, which had spread the older Greek civilisation through the ancient world, from our island in the north, through France, part of Spain and Italy in the south, to what is now Turkey and Egypt in the east. Greek civilisation never penetrated Germany— a very, very significant fact. It was a wonderful civilisation in many ways. It bound together a great society under one law and authority. In the fifth century the Barbarians—the Teutonic tribes from whom the Germany of to-day has descended—invaded and destroyed that ordered society, and reduced it to chaos. Schools were closed down, libraries were burnt, estates were ruined, and cities were destroyed. Anarchy and violence reigned supreme. "To-day there is on every side death, on every side grief, on every side desolation; on every side we are being smitten, on every side our cup is being filled with bitterness" (St. Gregory). That was written nearly 1,500 years ago.

The only power left, in that world of agony and anarchy, that could restore order and tame and civilise the barbarian, was the Church. The State had been destroyed, the armies broken, and the Civil Service smashed.

Only the Church was left, with her priests, monks, and Pope. And out of that rude, savage mass, the Church built a new civilisation, with glories that surpassed even those of Rome. The Church, with all her imperfections, did restore order and give security to Europe, for a period.

Now here is the question I should like to ask: How did it happen that there was a Church there at all? And how did it come about that the Church was able to survive in that flood of destruction and savagery? Well, the Church of the fifth century was the result of men becoming Christians in the fourth, third, right back to the first centuries. There was once a man named Saul—a really great man. He became a Christian. That is, he despaired of himself, and gave himself up to God. He was re-named Paul. He lived by the new nature and spirit, and was the means of others becoming Christian, who in turn influenced still others, and so on to the fifth century, when there was this power to lift society on to a new level of civilisation. Would there have been a fifth-century Church if there had been no Paul? I wonder! It is quite certain, however, that it was because men and women became Christians in the first century that the evil of the barbarian invasions in the fifth was restricted and checked.

"For I am not ashamed of the Gospel," said St. Paul, "for it is the power of God unto salvation. . . ." It is also, paradoxically enough, the power of God for the renewal of civilisation in our time, whatever crop of evils and problems the new civilisation may produce for our children. But here and now, Europe's direst need is for a generation of men who believe in Heaven, in an order of reality transcending time. Let individual Churchmen in their thinking, in their devotions, in their worship, be made more acutely aware of that other world, and they will be rendering to contemporary society a service similar to that rendered by the Church in the fifth century, over which had rolled, too, a barbarian flood. During this season of Lent, especially, let the outstanding thought in heart and mind be that great, triumphant utterance in the Apostle's Creed: "I BELIEVE ... in the forgiveness of sins AND THE LIFE EVERLASTING." From that belief in the life everlasting, if men really believe it, will spring a new temporal life, "a new birth of freedom, when government of the people, by the people, and for the people shall not perish from the earth."

QUESTIONS FOR STUDY CIRCLES

1. What assumptions about the nature and powers of collective humanity lie behind the modern idea of progress?

2. Does the history of war justify these assumptions?

3. What does modern psychology, with its revelation of widespread neurosis, indicate or suggest about the character of human nature?

4. In what way does the Christian view of man, as a sinner needing redemption by a power other than human nature itself, conflict with modern secular assumptions about man?

5. How would you state the character of the solution which Christianity offers to the problem of man's predicament in history, as that is revealed by war and psychological sickness?

6. What is the minimum, essential condition for the application of the Christian solution?

7. In what way is Christianity applicable to the whole life of man on earth?

8. Has it any immediate, urgent relevance to the present situation of a world in dire crisis?